THE GOOD STEPMOTHER

THE GOOD STEPMOTHER

A PRACTICAL GUIDE

Karen Savage and Patricia Adams

CROWN PUBLISHERS, INC.
NEW YORK

Grateful acknowledgment is given for permission to reprint selections from the following:

The Poetry of Robert Frost. Edited by Edward Connery Lathem. Copyright 1930, 1939, © 1969 by Holt, Rinehart and Winston, Inc. Copyright © 1958 by Robert Frost. Copyright © 1967 by Lesley Frost Ballantine. All rights reserved. Used by permission of Henry Holt and Company, Inc.

"Puberty and Parents" by Bruce A. Baldwin, Ph.D. Copyright © 1986 by Bruce A. Baldwin, Ph.D. All rights reserved. Used by permission of the author.

"The Stepfamily Cycle: An Experimental Model of Stepfamily Development" by Patricia Papernow. Copyright © 1984 by Patricia Papernow. All rights reserved. Used by permission of National Council on Family Relations.

Publisher's Note: This book contains case histories derived from interviews and research. The relevant facts have not been altered. However, names and other identifying details have been changed to protect the privacy of the individuals interviewed.

Published by Crown Publishers, Inc., 225 Park Avenue South, New York, New York 10003, and represented in Canada by the Canadian MANDA Group

CROWN is a trademark of Crown Publishers, Inc.

Manufactured in the United States of America

Library of Congress Cataloging-in-Publication Data

Savage, Karen.
    The good stepmother : a practical guide / Karen Savage, Patricia Adams.
        p.   cm.
    Bibliography: p.
    1. Stepmothers.   I. Adams, Patricia, 1942–   II. Title.
HQ759.92.S28   1988
306.8′743—dc 19   87-31859
ISBN 0-517-56731-8

Book design by Shari DeMiskey

10 9 8 7 6 5 4 3 2 1

First Edition

꩜

Contents

THE GOOD STEPMOTHER

Introduction

Iᴛ ɪs ᴀ ʙʟᴜsᴛᴇʀʏ ɴɪɢʜᴛ, ᴡɪᴛʜ ʀᴀɪɴ ᴀɴᴅ ᴡɪɴᴅ ʙʟᴏᴡɪɴɢ ᴡᴇᴛ ʟᴇᴀᴠᴇs against the windows. It is dark as only a November night can be. I am rushing around the kitchen with my daughter, Miranda, and husband, Lee, cleaning up after our hurried meal. I feel annoyed that I have to go out on such a miserable evening, but I tell myself that I have organized the meeting, so I have no one to blame but myself.

"I'm going to be late," I say, grabbing my coat from the coatrack and turning to Miranda. "Do you have a lot of homework?"

"A little," she shrugs, and her face lights up as the phone rings.

I hesitate at the kitchen door as Lee answers it.

"Oh hello!" he says, his voice slightly tentative. "Everything all right?"

I raise my eyebrows in question.

"It's Willy," Lee answers.

"Oh, how is he?" I ask. "Does he want to talk to me?"

1

"Karen is just on her way out," Lee says into the mouth-piece. "Do you want to . . . ?"

Lee stops. He shakes his head at me and waves me off.

I leave, and by the time I climb into the car, I can feel the wetness through my raincoat. It seems unlikely that anyone will come out on such a night. I think of how it would have been so much nicer back at home, where it was warm and I could have just put on a robe and sat by the fire and read.

As I pull the car away from the curb, I realize I have a slight lump in my throat. OK. I have to admit it. I'm hurt because Willy didn't seem to have anything to say to me. I've hardly spoken to him since last summer, when Lee and I visited him at his home on Martha's Vineyard. Willy, who is twenty-eight, has recently separated from his wife, and I know he is troubled, but I am reluctant to ask questions.

One day the three of us are on the beach. I am swimming while Willy and Lee sit in the sun. I have been out in the water a long time, and when I return to where they are, I jokingly shake water on Lee and then kneel down and give him a kiss. Out of the corner of my eye, I see Willy, looking at us. I pull back, feeling myself the intruder, the stepmother. I continue to have a sense that it is still hard for my stepchildren to accept their father's divorce, even though it's been over twenty years since it took place. In their sense of what is *right,* their father should be with their mother, not with me. Coming to terms with their parents' divorce is one of the hardest tasks children are ever faced with. As Oscar Wilde said, "Children begin by loving their parents; after a time they judge them; rarely, if ever, do they forgive them."

As I pull into the parking lot beside my office, I remember meeting Willy when he was an attractive eight-year-old; I was sure I would like him and very much wanted him to like me. I was convinced we would get along marvelously. It did not quite work out that way. It rarely does between stepmothers and stepsons.

Looking back, I realize that when I became a stepmother, I had no idea what role I was going to play, how I should act with my stepchildren, or how they would react to me. It was hard. Sometimes it seemed impossible, but it did not occur to me to seek help in those early years of stepmotherhood. Like so many stepmothers, I was unwilling to admit that we, as a family, really needed help.

I arrive at my office and turn up the heat, bring in some extra chairs, and turn on the lamp in the corner. I can hear the wind and rain. The room looks cheerful and comfortable enough, however, and I feel satisfied with the atmosphere I have worked to create. As a psychotherapist, I realize the need for a comfortable office where my patients can feel relaxed. I do a lot of family therapy, and my primary interest is stepfamilies.

I sit down at my desk and think again of Willy. Here I am, a psychotherapist waiting to conduct the monthly meeting of the Stepfamily Resource Center, an organization that I have founded through the Foundation for Religion and Mental Health in Briarcliff Manor, New York. With my education and my professional and personal experience, I am well equipped to answer questions and advise families who are having difficulties. And yet, when I imagine that my twenty-eight-year-old stepson might not want to speak to me on the phone, I get a lump in my throat. I feel rejected. I still, after all these years, want to be accepted by him. Being a stepmother is forever, and the emotions, hopes, and disappointments never end.

It was my involvement with my stepchildren that started me on the path that finally led me to family counseling, although it was drugs and prisons that initially concerned me.

When Willy and his older brother, Pete, were teenagers, I was constantly worried about drugs. It was the early 1970s, and I was well aware of the prevalence of drugs in the community. As a stepmother, I felt an unrealistic but nevertheless common concern that if my stepsons became involved with drugs, I would somehow be at fault.

When a close friend's son was arrested and sent to jail for selling marijuana, I immediately became involved with her situation. I volunteered to work with the probation office, and for a year I counseled two young women who were on probation. They both lived in stepfamilies. I was then asked to co-lead a group of parents whose children were on probation, and here too the majority of families were either single-parent or stepfamilies. I realized as I worked with these people that I wanted to make this occupation my profession and returned to graduate school to study.

In retrospect, I believe I studied psychology, and counseling also, as a way of getting help for myself and my family. There were no stepfamily resource centers then, and, except for private therapy, there were very few places to turn to for advice and counseling. A friend who had been a stepmother for over ten years returned to Alcoholics Anonymous for help, not knowing where else to go.

My graduate education helped me better to understand the dynamics of stepfamily life. It was not that I suddenly had all the answers, but I was able to step back a bit, let go, and be more objective. Even after I received my master's degree, however, I did not concentrate on family therapy. I began work as a psychotherapist with a counseling center doing individual therapy. One summer I worked for Westchester County, New York, setting up a "Prison Families Anonymous" program, researching prison policies and working with family members of people in jail.

It was exciting and challenging work, but in my psychotherapy practice I became increasingly aware that while many stepfamilies were seeking counseling, there was a paucity of services available to them. It was soon apparent to me that my real interest was in working not with prisoners and their families, but with another type of family in need of help—the stepfamily. I had been working for Hudson Shores Counseling Center, one of twelve counseling centers run by the Foundation for Religion and Mental Health; after two years of training in family therapy, I established the Stepfamily Resource Center.

On this particular November evening, I am preparing to conduct our monthly meeting. Everything is ready, but I know that it is possible that no one will show up—not because of the bad weather, but because even today, when one out of five kids in America lives in a stepfamily, there is still resistance to facing up to the problems and admitting that help is needed. I have conducted courses in stepfamily survival for adult-education programs, have spoken to numerous church and school groups, have conducted workshops for counseling centers and teachers' associations. The community at large is becoming aware of the difficulties of stepparenting. Still, I have found that most stepfamilies remain reluctant to air their problems. The sense of guilt and failure that often exists with stepparents keeps them from seeking counseling.

A single woman comes to the door. She is timid and worried that she has come to the wrong place. I assure her that she is in the right place, and she, apologetically, says that she has just come to listen and that her husband was unable to come with her. She has traveled forty-five minutes in pouring rain to attend this meeting, but she is clearly nervous at the prospect of our having a "one-on-one" situation.

Two more couples arrive almost simultaneously. All five people are in their mid-thirties and all attempt to convey an "I just stopped by to check this out" attitude as we sit down.

We introduce ourselves. The single woman is Eleanor. One couple gives their names as Fred and Lisa and explain that they are thinking about getting married. Fred has three children by a previous marriage, and Lisa has not been married before. The other couple are David and Lynn, and they have been married about three years, have one child of their own, and share custody of David's son by a previous marriage.

I explain that I have been a psychotherapist for the past five years, that I am also the director of the Stepfamily Resource Center, which is set up to address both the general community through seminars and workshops, and also to offer therapy, both group and individual, to those requesting help.

The evening's topic, which has been announced in the monthly newsletter, is "The Stepmother ... Witch or Saint?" I tell the group that as a stepmother for over twenty years, I have vacillated between the two images. I speak about my personal experiences briefly and then ask them how they are coping.

At first, everyone is reluctant to speak, but finally one of the women, Lynn, says that she really does feel that as a stepmother she has somehow slipped from being a saint to being a witch.

Lynn's husband, David, has said earlier that he has come to hear me speak specifically on this topic, and it is clear that he is angry about Lynn's treatment of Terry, his son by his first marriage.

Initially, Lynn and Terry got along extremely well, and established a very close bond. Lynn enjoyed mothering him and loved doing things with him. She took extra time to help him with homework, always looked for little extra gifts to give him, and cooked his favorite meals. But then, for no apparent reason, Terry became hostile, took everything she did for granted, never thanked her, and became demanding and surly. After she had her own son the situation worsened, and now she finds that she and Terry can hardly stand to be together at all. David feels that Lynn too obviously prefers their son and ignores Terry.

At this point, the second couple joins in. Fred says that Lynn and David's problem is exactly what he wants to avoid. He wants to be sure that if he and Lisa marry, they will have no children. He feels that the three children he already has deserve the best he has to offer. Another child would put them in second place. Lisa insists that it is unfair for him to expect her to give up her own chance at mothering for his and his children's sake.

Eleanor now feels comfortable enough to speak, and she explains that she is married to a man who lived alone with his son for three years before their marriage. She now has a baby, and her stepson, who is ten, acts so sullen and threatening toward her and her baby that she locks herself in her bedroom to avoid him when they are alone in the house together.

As I listen to these stories, I realize that although each situation is unique, each one is also a classic example of the problems of a stepfamily. I have heard these problems over and over.

Lynn's stepson clearly felt a conflict of loyalties because he liked Lynn so much that it made him feel disloyal to his mother. As he tried to distance himself from her, she felt hurt and reacted in a negative way. Fred expressed the fears that both stepchildren and stepparents have—of being relegated to second place by the closer bonds formed between biological parents and children. Eleanor was describing a classic example of the intense jealousy and anger of a young boy toward the woman and child who have replaced him in his father's life.

It is clear when our meeting is over that the two couples who arrived together would benefit from similar group meetings, while Eleanor and her family need individual counseling.

As I drive home, I think of Eleanor and the fear in her household. I am intrigued by her situation and glad that she has set up an appointment with me. I am anxious to meet her husband and hear how he views the situation. I realize that even though I hear these same stories again and again, I have never met a stepfamily that I have not found fascinating.

I pull up and see the lights of my home shining out into the rain. Up and down our street there are other lights, in other houses, all looking somewhat the same on this dark night. Just like the houses, each one of the families at the meeting is typical—I hear those problems regularly. But at the same time, just as inside each house there is a different family living its own life, each stepfamily I have seen tonight is unique. The entire range of human emotion is found in a stepfamily, an intricate, complex social unit that is rapidly becoming as common in our society as the nuclear family was in the past.

I think about the little group gathered in my office on this stormy night. All of them had come under the protective umbrella of a talk on stepmothers. A stepmother is the key to the stepfamily, and she is the most likely member of the family to seek help. If she can understand and deal with the particular problems of individuals living "in step," her family will have a much better chance. A stepmother needs group support, an understanding of what her stepchildren are experiencing, and practical advice, in order to find satisfaction in her role.

This book aims to provide such support through the accounts of other stepmothers. The women who speak in this book either have come to the counseling center for help or are women I have known personally. It is important for a stepmother to realize that her problems are shared by other stepmothers, and that one can expect hostility, anger, and frustration along with the pleasures and satisfactions of stepmotherhood.

Based on psychological studies and professional experience, this book will also explain the conflicts and traumas that children who live in stepfamilies experience. Intrinsic to a healthy relationship between a stepmother and her stepchildren is an understanding of their situation.

Understanding is only one aspect, however. As a stepmother once angrily said to me, "I *understand* why my stepdaughter took my shoes, but that doesn't get them back in my closet. I want to wear them!" There are ways to deal with the problems of stepmothering, and this book is written as a step-by-step guide, if you will, from the early stages of courtship until the children have left home.

A stepmother is sometimes "in step" with her role, and at other times she is "out of step." This book aims to provide a sense of group support and understanding by relating the experiences of other stepmothers, presents the viewpoint of the stepchildren, and gives sensible advice on how to make the role of stepmother as satisfying and fulfilling as possible. It is a practical guide, based on the knowledge that this is an imperfect world, and that there are no simple solutions. Each stepmother is unique, but if she understands both the limitations and the possibilities that can accompany her role, she will be more likely to find the satisfaction that will be beneficial to both her and her family.

1

Starting Out, Starting Over

In 1770, Samuel Johnson referred to remarriage as "the triumph of hope over experience." In 1966, when Lee and I decided to marry, experience certainly indicated that the odds were stacked against us. I was a divorced woman with two children, and Lee was still embroiled in a bitter divorce struggle, with his three children caught in the middle. Nevertheless, we hoped that our marriage would result in a happy combined family. We did not consider, however, the complexity of this combination. Our marriage would create an immediate family of seven people, all of whom would play several roles. I would be a wife, mother, and stepmother; Lee a husband, father, and stepfather; and our children would be brothers and sisters as well as stepbrothers and stepsisters. The children would have natural mothers and fathers and stepmothers and stepfathers. Since Lee and I intended to have our own children, they would have and would be half brothers and half sisters. In our family ex-spouses would play a role, as well as ex-spouses' relatives. Yet we hoped, and believed, that this variety of people, and the variety of roles we would play, would somehow fuse together into a happy family. It could only have been hope that propelled us forward into the unknown experiences of a stepfamily.

Over the years we have lived together and lived separately, loved one another and fought bitterly. There has been envy, hate, jealousy, and anger. There has also been compassion, hope, and love. These aspects of our family life continue. We are still a family, although dispersed, and our relationships with one another change and develop perpetually. And through all our experiences we have managed to forge a strong family unit.

I like to think of our family as being on a long and sometimes treacherous voyage, a voyage that has carried us through birth and death, arrivals and departures, togetherness and separation. The voyage has left some scars, but it has also left us with our destinies fused and our commitment to one another intact.

Now, Lee and I have come full circle. We were lovers, then stepparents in a stepfamily, then alone with our two children as a traditional nuclear family, and now, with our youngest daughter soon to go away to school, we will be alone together for the first time in our lives. We did it. We survived—but more than that—our lives have been given a depth and texture that would not have been possible without our mixed family.

It has taken time to realize this, however. I have a memory of a hot June day in 1967. I am picking up my three stepchildren to bring them into New York for the weekend. My own two children, aged seven and nine, are with me. As usual, we wait outside the rambling, comfortable suburban house where Lee used to live, and I honk the horn. I do not go inside. My status as intruder in the lives of the people who live there is made obvious by the fact the children always come out alone. I suspect their mother does not want to see me; my eight-month's-pregnant belly underlines the fact that she has lost her husband. I feel that as far as she's concerned, I now have stolen everything from her, including her position as sole mother of his children.

As I wait, I work to suppress the shrill accusations that I imagine these children have heard for the past three years. I am the "other woman," a family wrecker, immoral, selfish . . . the archetypal stepmother.

The children avert their eyes as they climb into the car. They are tempted and fascinated by the idea of a baby, but the fact that I am pregnant emphasizes the permanence of my relationship with their father and makes it harder for them to continue daydreaming about their parents getting back together again. There is also a more elemental fear. Will their father go on loving them now that he has another family, another child that is his? They are no longer innocent; they know that people can stop loving each other. If it could happen once, it can happen again.

As I drive down the West Side Highway the heat reflected off the pavement enters the car in almost palpable waves. The old station wagon is full; I am tired, hot, and uncomfortable. The children squirm impatiently in the back seat. Each of us dreads the coming weekend, this forced being together that feels unnatural to all of us. I dread the noise, the turbulent feelings that wash back and forth through the apartment all weekend, leaving my husband and me so emotionally drained that we fall wearily into what we have grown to call "The Sunday Night Fight."

My children dread sharing their rooms, their things, their claim on Lee as their father. They know that these other children are really his. After having him to themselves for five days, they must immediately relinquish their place.

My stepchildren dread spending time with me. I am the person closest to their father, whom they adore. I have awesome power. (They have been told that it was I, single-handedly, who broke up their parents' marriage.) I am determinedly pleasant, I never raise my voice, but I know that I could easily harbor the same feelings of confusion and bitterness against them that they harbor against me. I am a stepmother, after all.

Suddenly the car in front of me stops. I barely avoid a crash by jamming on my brakes, and all the children lurch

forward. Kate, my five-year-old stepdaughter, hits her forehead against the ashtray on the back of the seat, and I hear a
wail of pain. I am in a line of cars that is slowly moving
forward, horns are blowing, the heat beats up into our crowded
car. I quickly turn to see the blood rolling down from a cut
above her eye. Her face is filled with fear and hurt, and as I
frantically search for something to wipe off the blood, my
eleven-year-old stepson, Willy, wails.

"I'm going to throw up!"

"Here, Pete, quick," I say to the older stepson, handing
him a T-shirt from a basket of clean laundry that I had picked
up on my way out to get the children. "Help your sister. See
how bad the cut is."

"I can't make it!" Willy moans, but he does ... or almost
does.

The smell of vomit, the sound of crying (by now my
seven-year-old daughter Kris has begun to cry also, and my
son Nicky is worried about the automobile horns he believes
are all intended for us), the heat, the fumes, the insistent blare
of horns make me want to cry and scream out.

When we arrive at the apartment, I am weary to the bone.
As the children open the doors and run up to greet their father,
who has shouted a cheerful hello from the window, I simply
want to cry. I am too hot, too tired, too guilt-ridden. Let them
show him my latest failure, my latest debacle. Perhaps they
will convince him that I am indeed a wicked stepmother.

As I sit in the car, I think about how I had once believed
we could make anything work. But this family-that-refuses-to-
be-a-family is defeating us. How did we stray so far from the
pleasant dreams we had when we began living together to the
depressing disharmony of this, our stepfamily? What went
wrong? Is it possible that I *am* turning into a wicked stepmother?

When I remarried in 1966, it did not even occur to me that
I was becoming a stepmother. I was marrying Lee. For the
preceding five years we had both been so obsessed with each
other and with our struggle to be together that what our life
would be like when we actually were together had not even

seemed like something to worry about. In fact, the reality that we both had children had seemed incidental. We were getting married, not our children. We had agreed that my two kids would live with us and that his would visit every other weekend and for a month in the summer. I was aware that Lee had suffered terribly during the two years he had been living away from his family. He adored his children, and separation from them was the most painful experience he had ever been through. We both counted on the fact that once we had a home together, the children would be as happy as we were. They were close in age, they knew each other, and there didn't seem to be any reason we couldn't all get along beautifully. Naively, we believed that living in a stepfamily would be just like living in any other family. None of our friends had gotten divorced or remarried as yet; I didn't know anyone else who was a stepparent, but I didn't see any reason why it should be any different from being a parent, and I loved that. Lee's children were charming and attractive, and so far they had always been pleasant and cheerful to be with. Our children were so important to us that we wanted to share the experience of having a child together as soon as possible.

Unfortunately, we started making mistakes immediately. Our first mistake was the marriage ceremony itself. Although I had obtained a divorce in 1963 and Lee and I had lived together since June of 1965, by the spring of 1966 Lee had still been unable to obtain a divorce. In March of 1966, as a last resort, he decided to get a unilateral divorce in Mexico, which in effect is a divorce without spousal consent. This made it necessary for us to marry in Mexico. Our lawyer advised us to get the divorce and marry immediately after, and to inform family members when it was a fait accompli.

When we told my children, their reaction was ecstatic. I had been divorced for over three years, and since their father had moved to California they rarely saw him. They lived with Lee and me in our New York apartment and were aware of our plans. They were pleased to have Lee as their stepfather.

Lee's children reacted differently. Their silence when he told them was completely unexpected. We had assumed that our marriage would be a relief rather than a threat to them. Our telling them only after our marriage was a big mistake, however. It made them feel that something had been put over on them. Instead of trying to make them a part of our life together, we had made them feel that they were being pushed out of their father's life.

We were living in Greenwich Village at the time, and they soon were insisting that they didn't want to come in to the city on weekends. We bought a house in the country, hoping that it would provide more neutral territory for us to be together. On Fridays we would pack up the car, my kids, groceries, and supplies, then travel an hour to pick up Lee's three children and another hour to our country house. Almost five hours every weekend spent in a crowded car with the kids squirming, punching each other, and wanting to go to the bathroom . . . all so we could spend a weekend sorting out squabbles—between his and mine, between mine, between his, and, more and more often, between us.

I don't think I consciously thought of myself as a step-mother during those years. I can remember setting attainable goals for myself, like having a hot nutritious meal on the table within an hour after our arrival, or making sure each child had his or her own bed with special covers and pillow. Overall, however, I didn't really have any clear idea of what my relationship with Lee's children should be. Whatever role I tried to play never seemed to fit. Whoever I tried to be made me feel uncomfortable. I was either trying too hard to please and getting rejected, or giving up and hiding from my stepchildren—they often seemed to be everywhere—up in my room with a book, or sneaking a few hours of peace on Sunday morning at the laundromat.

Most of the time, my stepsons, who were ten and eleven when Lee and I were married, ignored me. If they did look at me, they quickly averted their eyes as though I were too bright. I probably was. As my anxiety grew, I babbled on at them, endlessly trying to make friends, cooking what I thought were wonderful meals, trying to coax everything into being alright. It simply didn't work. Nothing we did together felt natural, and I was always aware that they would not have chosen to be with me if they had been given a choice, and that only natural politeness made them tolerate me at all. I soon felt that I would prefer not spending time with them either, although I knew they were, for others, immensely likable. Between us, however, there was always an unspoken undercurrent. . . . They had made it clear from the beginning that on some level I was the enemy, and the enemy I remained.

My stepdaughter Kate was easier, since she was born close to the time her parents' marriage broke up and did not remember living with her father. She had a naturally sunny nature, and she and my six-year-old daughter, Kris, were close in age and for the most part got along well.

My eight-year-old son Nicky liked his stepbrothers, but their preadolescence coupled with their hostility toward me inevitably surfaced when the boys were together. One day Nicky came running into the kitchen, his face confused and angry.

"Mommy, Pete and Willy said that you and Lee do *it* all the time, and I told them it wasn't true, you wouldn't do that. Please tell them you don't so they'll stop talking about it."

"But, Nicky," I tried to explain, openly but gently, "Lee and I do make love. We are married and we love each other. Making love is a natural expression of that love."

He looked at me in astonishment. Nicky obviously shared Pete and Willy's feelings of wrong about my sleeping with their father. Lee and I still did not belong together in their version of how things should be. Children tend not to think of their parents as sexual beings, but when Mommy or Daddy is in bed with someone else, even a stepparent, the sexuality of the relationship is not so easily avoided by the child. It would take years for our marriage to be real to all the children.

I often despaired, afraid that I was the problem. All the children loved Lee, but around me Lee's boys were apt to be monosyllabic. I could not help but believe that this would eventually harm my relationship with Lee, and I knew how he tried to protect me. One frosty morning, when I went out to the outhouse, I found "I hate Karen" scrawled on the wall. I crept back into bed next to Lee, too hurt to say anything. The next time I went out, it was gone. It took two days for Lee to tell me that he had seen it and removed it; the whole subject was almost too painful for us to talk about, even with each other. A pervasive sense of failure hung over us; we were unable to create a family.

I continued to feel myself the outsider. One weekend Willy fell out of a tree and got a nasty wound in his foot. I rushed him to the doctor and stood by him as the doctor probed his wound for splinters. Willy held my hand desperately but at the same time glared at me accusingly as the pain became too much and he started to cry. I felt he was blaming me for not being someone else. I felt like an intruder, forced, against his will, to witness the intimacy of his pain. Afterward we both felt embarrassed, like strangers who have overstepped the bounds of their relationship and now don't know how to go back to being strangers.

We continued to be together, an unwilling and often recalcitrant group, every other weekend and for one month in the summer. A degree of familiarity, born of a hundred small contacts, crept into our relationship almost imperceptibly. There were times when we began to feel like a family. I remember how the children would spend hours building things together—intricate villages with pebble streets and moss roofs, tree houses, forts of tree branches cut and angled carefully for shelter. I felt we were all building, building a place for ourselves in each others' lives. There were quiet evenings when Lee and I would lie in bed and think that the day hadn't gone too badly, considering.

These times were still interspersed with days when we were both in despair, but the despair began to seem more manageable. After one particularly difficult weekend, we visited a friend who was a psychiatrist. We asked him how long Lee's children would continue to have angry feelings about me. To our surprise, he told us that we could expect such feelings to last through childhood, through adolescence, and into early adulthood. He assured us that we were not necessarily doing anything wrong; the resentment and anger was natural and would take time to work itself out. Even though we knew we were in for a long haul, his words lifted an enormous burden from us. We did not have to accomplish everything now, we could relax.

Time, birth, and death ultimately forged us into a real family. In July 1967, we had a son, Adam. His birth was the first event in the family that was greeted with joyous enthusiasm by everybody. Adam was lively and communicative from the moment he was born, and all the children took turns carrying him around, begging to feed him and to play with him. We felt more related, and in truth we were at least truly related to one another through Adam. Our being together didn't seem like such a pretense. Adam adored all his brothers and sisters; his sunny approval made me feel closer to them, and now we had one subject, endlessly interesting, that was always safe to talk about. Lee and I also found it wonderful to have one child about whom we felt no conflict; we could admire him equally—he was *ours*. In fact, he was so much admired that I often felt that I didn't get enough time alone with him. I used to look forward to the 2 A.M. feeding because it was the only chance I got to be with him at my leisure. I loved those moments, the house quiet around us, milky closeness, peace and contentment flowing between us. Pictures taken during Adam's first years of life show him almost always in the middle of his doting family, smiling cheerfully, almost as though he were a small ambassador bringing two wary countries together.

It was a time when we were all filled with hope. Everything seemed possible—we were going to be a big, happy family after all.

But fate struck us an almost unbearable blow. On a Fourth of July family picnic, my son Nicholas, who was then ten, drowned accidentally. The tragedy struck us all to the core. Each one of us, including Willy and Pete, worried that we might have done something to prevent Nicky's death. And yet no one assigned blame. We somehow managed to get through the rest of the summer and even to keep the house, where we learned, day by day and month by month, to accept and live with what had happened. Shared grief was not the strongest emotion that drew us together, but it was one of the many emotions and life experiences that built the feelings of familiarity and fondness our family shares.

The following year, Lee and I had a baby girl, Miranda. By 1969 our family was comprised of Lee's two sons Pete and Willy, his daughter Kate, my daughter Kristin, and the two children we had had together, Adam and Miranda.

Just as the psychiatrist had predicted, my stepsons mellowed considerably toward me as they reached their late teens. Both of them moved in with us for varying lengths of time, and as they were too old to require any sort of mothering, we circled each other emotionally until we discovered just the right balance of closeness and distance. I really liked having them around and found that they had developed into intelligent, interesting, and independent young men. They in turn appreciated the freedom we gave them. I was able to share our home with them without putting pressure on them, other than expecting them to contribute financially if they were working or to be responsible for their studies if they were in school. In some ways I became easier to be around than if I had been their natural mother, and they began to see me as a separate person, no longer encumbered with the prejudices and angers they had felt earlier. They could also see that our marriage was a happy one and that our family circle was a pleasant place to be. And they belonged: not the way they did at their mother's house, which would always be their primary hearth, but with a degree of ease and a feeling of acceptance that were clearly important to them. We found we could express affection genuinely, which would have been impossible ten years earlier.

Sometimes it seemed, however, that when certain relationships in the family improved, others became more difficult. My daughter Kris grew restless and unhappy as a teenager. She and Lee were constantly at odds, natural enough between daughter and father but more complicated between a daughter and stepfather. I was busy with Lee's and my two young children and with trying to work things out with my stepchildren, and Kris was in many ways alone. I was the only "complete" relation she had in the house. There were times

when the tension between Lee and Kris was so great that I
wondered if I should leave with her, but I knew deep down that
this was no solution. Kris was separating from the family, as
teenagers do, and it was my job to be supportive but at the
same time to remain steadfast in my commitment to my
marriage. Kris, with her father's financial support, decided to
go to boarding school when she was sixteen. Although I was
upset at her decision, I realized that all the members of a
stepfamily must work out their lives in their own particular
ways and that being a stepmother can change the way a mother
relates to her own children.

　　Kate, my stepdaughter, moved in with us when she was
sixteen and lived with us for three years. I had some appre-
hension about how we would adjust to each other. Although we
had always gotten along fairly well, she was now in full
adolescent rebellion against her mother, and I was not sure
what my role would be. Kate was a naturally friendly and
ebullient girl, however, and had always instinctively mothered
Lee's and my children, Adam and Miranda. Miranda was
thrilled to have another big sister in the house, and she
modeled herself after Kate, trying on her makeup and fixing
her hair like her big sister. Kate taught her feminine skills that
I wasn't very good at, and as I watched I realized the benefits
of our mixed family. Miranda had many different models for
womanliness, and Kate was able to have a younger sister she
could advise and enjoy. Kate settled into a relaxed relationship
not only with the immediate family, but with my many aunts,
uncles, and cousins as well. She called my mother "Grandmother" and gave me birthday and Christmas cards addressed
to her "other mother."

　　Nevertheless, although I missed Kate when she moved out
after three years with us, I also experienced an almost imper-
ceptible easing of feeling in the household. It took me a few
weeks to figure out why: for the first time in sixteen years of
marriage, Lee and I were living alone with our own children.
It was lovely to have his and mine visit, but after all those
years of being a stepfamily it was even lovelier to be a nuclear
family.

Our son Adam has left home for college now, and our daughter Miranda will soon do the same. We have come full circle. It is over twenty years since I fell in love with Lee and hoped and dreamed of being only with him. That day has been a long time in coming, but the years we have spent together as parents and stepparents have deepened our relationship and enlarged our capacity for love and understanding. We will always be a stepfamily, however. Now the children visit rather than live in, and these visits are full of color and emotion. My stepchildren have enriched my life immeasurably; they have taught me a great deal about myself and my capacity to survive. They have made me realize that there is no one perfect role for the stepmother to play. The very essence of the step-relationship is its fluidity, its chameleonlike ability to change according to what is possible and desirable at the moment for both stepchild and stepmother. I have had a lot of wicked thoughts as a stepmother, but I have had far more loving ones. Most of all, I have learned to accept the step-relationship for what it is rather than for what I think it should be.

I wish I had known some of these truths when I set out on my own stepfamily journey. I had to learn, painfully and slowly. There were no guidelines to follow, no signposts pointing out potential danger spots, no checklists to tell me whether I was doing well or failing completely.

A stepfamily can be a wonderful, rich, and fulfilling experience. It can also become a nightmare for the stepparent who expects it to be just like a biological family. The stepfamily's strength and vitality lie in its differentness, and trying to force it to behave like a biological family can spell certain disaster.

Looking back, I can see the mistakes we made, and experience and education in the field have given me a certain objectivity as I relate our family's history. But it is not just history—our family is still a stepfamily, and I find that nothing is ever finished or settled. The complexity of our relationships will shift and vary as we move through the various stages of our lives. I, as a stepmother, will never move completely away from vulnerability and a desire to make everything work out. I will still suffer disappointments and frustrations.

Nevertheless, I still experience a real sense of excitement when I hear a couple deciding to combine their families and live in step. Even though a stepfamily's journey is one fraught with peril, it is also one filled with particular joys that enrich and deepen one's life. It *is* a living example of hope triumphing over experience.

2

Before the Marriage

WHO'S THAT KNOCKING ... TAP, TAP,
TAPPING ON OUR BEDROOM DOOR?

TOLSTOY WAS WRONG. ALL HAPPY FAMILIES DO NOT RESEMBLE ONE
another. Some happy families are stepfamilies, and they do not
usually resemble happy nuclear families. This is an important
fact for a woman to remember as she tries to understand what
it means to be a stepmother. Even the pattern of courtship is
different for a woman who forms a relationship with a father.
It is never simple—it is never "boy meets girl" but rather
woman meets man, and man's children, and sometimes man's
ex-wife, ex-in-laws.... It's a package deal.

Single fathers have children who have been through a loss
and who are often vulnerable and wary. Add to this a woman's
own emotional baggage from her family of origin, and from her
own past marriage if she has been married or from her single
life-style if she has not, and one can see that each situation is
too special to be "normal" or "typical." The fact is that a
stepfamily is a family born of loss, and therefore each stepfamily must find its own unique way to be happy, and each happy
stepfamily will be happy in its own way.

Our individual behavioral patterns are initially formed by what we feel and observe in our family of origin. I grew up in a big extended family where I was influenced not only by my own parents but also by my various aunts and uncles. I was able to see how differently married people acted, how some got along and others fought, but generally how they remained committed to their spouse. Divorce was rarely an option, and I grew up assuming that I would spend my life married to one person.

I got married the summer after my college graduation, moving from my father's house into my husband's. It was a small wedding; I was the typical virgin bride, and my new husband was handsome, witty, intelligent, and bound, one hoped, for great things. From the outside we were an enviable couple, but inside the marriage, almost from the start, there was an absence of deep feeling. I felt lonely all the time. After a few years we had become only distant friends and even the births of our two children, Nicholas and Kristin, had not really brought us closer together. My husband seemed constantly dissatisfied, and I was frustrated and confused, unable to make things any better. To some extent I accepted our relationship because I knew no other.

Lee and I had known each other in childhood. We met again when we both moved into the same suburban community with our families. Lee's marriage was troubled, but he was a man obviously committed to his family. Our attraction manifested itself at first in acceptable ways; we met openly in social situations. But we found ourselves remaining at the dinner table at dinner parties, talking until it was time to leave, or separating ourselves from the crowd at cocktail parties or picnics. In spite of the growing intensity of our attraction, we did not meet secretly or even verbally express our feelings for months. I was a good girl, after all—a married woman, the mother of two children. It was 1961, and the so-called sexual revolution was still no more than a distant rumbling.

My reluctance to become more deeply involved with Lee was very real, because I feared that I would be held responsible for our actions even though we had both made the decision. I

knew that I would be the "other woman" but that he would not
be the "other man." Nevertheless, we fell into the situation in
which so many "illicit" lovers find themselves, caught up in one
another, sneaking, lying, and trying to see each other without
hurting our respective families. This situation is not uncommon for people who are in the process of leaving their
marriage, and it can be a turbulent and destructive time for all
involved. I had no doubts about my feelings for Lee, but
nevertheless my sense of guilt about our behavior was painful.
I was going against the teachings and convictions of my family
background, in which there had only been one divorce. Women
who have become involved with a married man, as I did, begin
their stepmother journey already cast into a mold that implies
wickedness. Even today, society tends to view the woman as
keeper of the hearth, and when a woman has an affair with a
married man she tends to carry the brunt of societal disap-
proval. When we finally did become lovers, I almost felt that I
should wear a scarlet *A* upon my chest. This sense of guilt
made me especially vulnerable during the period of separation
and divorce, after Lee and I had agreed to tell our spouses and
to try to plan a life together.

In 1963 we both left our spouses and moved into separate
apartments in New York City. Lee's separation from his
children, however, proved much harder than we had supposed.
My divorce was relatively simple and almost amicable. Lee
struggled with his separation for a long time.

During this three-year period between marriages I had a
part-time job. I was trying to be a single parent and cope with
two young children in New York City, pay my bills, and sort
out what was happening to my life. I was often in doubt about
my decisions, often hurt and angry at Lee, worried about my
children, and, in general, anxious about not making another
mistake with my life that would cause suffering to myself and
others.

This painful period of separation and divorce happens to
almost every woman who becomes a stepmother and is part of
the baggage she brings with her into her next marriage.

No matter how a woman eventually resolves her divorce, it

represents, for a period of time at least, a failure, a "failed" marriage. As children growing up, none of us expect our marriage to end in divorce, and our expectations and views of marriage are often formed by observing our parents and relatives. If we have observed strife and unhappiness, we hope to avoid it. If we have observed commitment and love, we hope to copy it. In either case, we have failed.

A woman who has experienced divorce is therefore often wounded and wary. She is trying to find her own identity and independence. If she has children, she is forming a new and different relationship with those children, and this takes time and effort on her part.

Single women who are considering marriage to a man with children are also making enormous changes in their lives. Usually they have a profession and enjoy a certain amount of freedom and independence. If they have thought of marriage, it has probably been with the idea of marrying a single man and having a family with him. Marriage to a father is a very different thing indeed.

Although a single woman has not suffered the traumas of divorce, she probably has had little or no mothering experience, and to marry not only a man, but a family as well, demands major adjustments.

A woman I know, Mary Beth, had worked hard to send herself to school and to get a degree in nursing. After working in a hospital for a number of years she decided that she wanted to enjoy her single life, to travel and see the world. She became an airline stewardess and met Daniel soon afterward. Daniel was divorced with one son, who had suffered from an unusual childhood disease that had caused both medical and emotional problems. Although Mary Beth fell in love with Daniel, she did not feel ready to take on his son's problems. The child needed a lot of financial and emotional support, and she had to decide if she was willing to include him in her life. For a time she felt angry; the demands of the child were too great. She had had no part in his early development, and now she felt that she had to deal with an almost untenable situation. The courtship, which could have been spent having exciting weekends in Paris, was spent driving miles for Daniel's son's medical treatments. Instead of a carefree life of travel and fun, Mary Beth would take on the responsibilities of "instant mother." She simply had to decide whether or not Daniel was worth the price. She decided he was, but there was never a time in their courtship and eventual marriage when it was "just the two of them." Daniel's son was always a part of their relationship, whether or not he was with them physically.

When a woman becomes involved with a father, the inevitable moment comes when she is to meet his children. She is almost always anxious for them to like her. Although her intentions are the best and the children may also feel the need to please, "Daddy's friend" can often be a target for their anger or hurt. If their father is single they have experienced a loss, and very often these children are suffering. There are few people, children or adults, who can go through divorce or death without having difficulty in starting a new series of relationships.

Children whose families have been disrupted are in pain. In Joan B. Kelly and Judith S. Wallerstein's study on children and divorce, a young boy described his parents' divorce by saying, "It's splitting me in two." To emphasize his dilemma, he drew his hand hatchet-style down the middle of his forehead. Wallerstein and Kelly go on:

> The child frequently perceives the parent's departure as a departure from *him*, personally. In addition, the physical departure of the parent and the parent's belongings, and the continuing absence of this parent, makes the family disruption undeniably real. This experience precipitates a spectrum of responses which may or may not be observable to the parent. In this respect, the central event of divorce for children is psychologically comparable to the event of death, and frequently evokes similar responses of disbelief, shock, and denial.[1]

These children's attempts to cope with loss can be made even more difficult by the presence of another love figure in their father's life. Even if their father has been separated from their mother for a long period of time, the children have at least had him more or less to themselves, and they will naturally resent the intrusion of a woman in their life together.

From 1963 until 1965, when Lee and I were separated from our previous spouses but living apart, I was regularly confused about my role with his children. They came to visit him in New York on weekends, in his own apartment, and so I was not immediately placed in a mothering position. We did all spend time together, however, with our combined five children, going to the Central Park Zoo or taking short trips to the country. His boys often resented me and my children, since they wanted to see their father, not that woman and her two children. We were a threat, and we interfered with the time they wanted to spend alone with him.

Not all of the time we spent together during this period was unpleasant, and we could occasionally laugh and enjoy each other's company. Nevertheless, I evoked, at least on some levels, the primal fear of stepmothers that has been expressed in fairy tales and legends. It is the fear of loss, the loss first of one's mother but of the father as well. Every woman who becomes a stepmother is dealing with this sense of loss. The child has lost his or her family, either through divorce or death. By the time a stepmother comes into the child's life, his or her most basic, fundamental source of security has been disrupted.

The stepmother is often seen as a threat, for she represents a new, unknown order, and in the child's eye she has not only in some fashion replaced the biological mother, but she is often perceived as taking the father away as well. In "Hansel and Gretel" and in some versions of "Snow White" the father is rendered helpless by the strength of the wicked stepmother. She has replaced the child's nurturing, secure parents with a single tyrannical shrew who is bent on destroying her stepchildren. If the wicked stepmother has children of her own, as in "Cinderella," then she will always push the stepchild back into the darkness, so that the light will shine only on her own.

These tales, which have survived centuries, can be found

in some form in cultures as diverse as the Chinese, Indian, and Eskimo. The stepmother tale predominates, however, in societies where the tribal culture is not so strong. In tribal cultures there were often laws that prevented a man from marrying outside his tribe or family group, thereby ensuring that a stepmother would have preexisting family or tribal ties to her stepchildren.

In our grandparents' generation the custom and often the necessity of a man marrying his deceased wife's sister was not uncommon. Divorce was rare, and any woman who was seen as the cause of a divorce was practically ostracised by society. In our present-day society, therefore, where it is now predicted that by the turn of the century one in two children will live in a stepfamily, there is little positive precedent for stepfamilies, and the very term "stepmother" traditionally carries with it the most negative of connotations.

Many of the children's fears are quite valid. They will have to share their father's love and attention with a stepmother and perhaps step-siblings, and they will have to let go of the fantasy that their parents will get back together.

Therapists who work with families going through a divorce note that the children in these families become more accident-prone than before and are much more likely to "act out" and get in trouble in school. These are methods by which the child is either trying to get attention or attempting to force the parents to come together in order to solve his or her problems. During the time it takes younger children to adjust to divorce they often dream and hope that their parents will be reunited and may try to make it happen.

Nathaniel, whose parents were separated and whose father was living with a woman with two small children, was a fullback on his soccer team. He and his father had played soccer together since he was four and the sport had been a great source of pleasure for them both. When his father brought his new friend and her children to his soccer games, however, Nathaniel was furious. He was convinced they knew nothing about the game and only interfered with his father's ability to watch him. He twisted and badly sprained his ankle during a

game and was out for the season. Even though there is no way
to prove that the sprained ankle was anything more than an
accident, there is ample evidence that children in these circumstances are accident prone because of their sense of frustration and helplessness in the face of their parents' divorce.

These children who are struggling with their own emotional problems are, unavoidably, a part of the adult courtship.
On the other hand, the adult couple are usually newly in love,
and the intensity of their feelings is as much a part of their
lives as their concern for the children. They want to be
together, they want to be alone. They are often sexually active,
and this aspect of their relationship is a source of both
curiosity and anxiety for the children.

Children are usually able to dismiss their biological
parents' sexuality and to transfer sexual fantasies toward
distant or impersonal figures. Certainly before puberty and
often even afterward, it is simply discomfiting for children to
think of their parents actually having sexual intercourse. But
if daddy is in bed with a woman who is not their mother, the
reality intrudes upon the children's minds.

In *Shoot the Moon,* a film that deals a couple's separation
and its effect on their family, the little girls curiously ask their
father's new lover about her making love with him. She tells
them it's like "eating ice cream," and the children toss and
wriggle down in their beds, giggling nervously at the idea. The
point here is simply that these children would rarely form the
question about their natural parents, but when a new person
appears to be intimate with their father, they need to deal with
his sexuality one way or another.

Preadolescents are particularly sensitive to these situations. They are at the most vulnerable age, an age when they
are becoming sexually aware and are sifting out sexual feelings
for their own parents and transferring them to other figures.

An eight-year-old boy, Eric, whose father left his mother
to live with another woman, spends every other weekend with
his father. He recently reported to his mother that he didn't
want to visit Daddy anymore because he got so cold at night.
As his mother questioned him, she realized that he had wet his

bed. "If that happens again," she said, "you just have to go tell Daddy and he will get you some dry sheets."

"But I'm not allowed in Daddy and CeCe's bedroom," he answered, shaking his head solemnly.

"But surely, if you need something?"

"No! Never, never, ever!"

The mother was so upset that she confronted her estranged husband with this information, only to find out that no such rule had been made. Eric had found his father's sleeping with CeCe so traumatic that he had begun wetting the bed again and could not bring himself even to enter the room where they slept.

The reaction of the children puts the dating couple in a difficult position. Some couples attempt to hide the fact that they are sexually involved, but children are wise to what is happening around them and feel even more alienated if they are lied to. Hal tried to hide the fact that he was involved with Christine and asked her not to visit when his sons were there. Not only was this offensive to Christine, it didn't even work. His sons found ample evidence of her cosmetics, hair conditioner, tampons, and other personal items that could only mean that their father was essentially living with a woman.

Christine insisted on being open about their relationship, but she was caught off guard when Hal's fifteen-year-old son arrived for the weekend with his young girlfriend, whom he introduced as his "lover." He had described his father's home as a "neat pad, where we can all crash together." When Hal insisted that he couldn't "crash" there with his girlfriend, his son answered with a surly smile, "Oh, do we make *you* uncomfortable?"

Women who are involved with fathers have undefined roles. They do not have any patterns to work from during this period of courtship. Nothing is fixed, and it is difficult both to be honest and at the same time to maintain a certain dignity.

More often than not, women want to like and be liked by their lover's children. They do not see themselves as intruders and are willing to do almost anything to become a part of the "family." At least initially.

Susan, who was a single woman in her thirties, met Frank, a divorced man with three children ranging in age from seven to fifteen. She knew that Frank's previous marriage had been traumatic and that his ex-wife was a very nervous woman whose home was chaotic. Frank, therefore, tried to create a sense of calm and peacefulness when his children visited him on weekends. He rented a farmhouse in the country, and his daughter, Rebecca, assumed a mothering role even though she was only thirteen. She and her father made fantastic meals for the whole family, and they were all very casual about bedtimes or other household rules. By the time Susan met Frank, the family had established their weekend routine.

Susan looked forward to meeting Frank's children. She planned to make chocolate-drop cookies with Rebecca, had brought books for the youngest boy, and hoped to look good playing touch football with them all.

The weekend was a disaster. Rebecca refused to speak to anyone on the drive up to the country and then went off to her room immediately. Frank was disappointed that his two "favorite women" had not hit it off, and his sons lurked about, refusing to go to bed. He suddenly felt uncomfortable about Susan and apologetically asked her to sleep in with Rebecca, whose room had twin beds.

Susan's relationship with Frank did not survive. After only a few months of trying to befriend this hard-core group, she decided that, as she put it, "Nothing is worth *that*."

Susan wanted a happy marriage, a loving relationship with her husband and his children, and she hoped to participate in their lives in the most positive way. She wanted to befriend the children, help them get over the trauma of their parents' divorce, and help them mature into happy, productive adults. Not such unrealistic expectations on the surface, but almost impossible under the circumstances. She felt frustrated, disliked, and a failure when in fact her only "fault" was that she had unrealistic expectations. She could not have seen that she would be considered an intruder in the bond that had developed between Frank and his children, especially Rebecca, who had taken on the role of substitute wife and mother. They did not want her, they were getting along just fine without her, and they resented even the slightest intrusion into their lives. Frank was not strong enough to assert his commitment to Susan and allowed his children to call the shots.

Children, however, be they teenagers or preschoolers, are never really comfortable if they are able to manipulate the adults around them. As Jean and Veryl Rosenbaum state in their book *Stepparenting*:

> Whenever children sense that adults are placating them, they feel uncomfortable and thus become more demanding. It also puts them one up on the manipulation scale.... Young people know they should not have so much power over an adult, so placating parents lose both the child's respect and their own authority.[2]

On the other hand, women who are trying to work out a sensible relationship with their lover's children need to recognize their own emotions, as well as those of the children. The Rosenbaums advise:

> Weekend stepparents may also be alarmed by the intensity of jealous feelings they feel toward the children. It is rather embarrassing to be jealous of a mere child. If you fall into the green pit, try to pull back a bit and rethink the situation. Remember that the child is probably in turn jealous of you because he has to share his parent with you.[3]

It was interesting to see that not long after Susan left, Frank became involved with a divorced woman, Martha, whom he had known a long time. She had two teenagers of her own and had no illusions about making Frank's children love her immediately. She asserted herself calmly but firmly and although there was initial resentment and hostility, she finally established a structure in which the combined families, five children in all, were able to work out a successful stepfamily relationship. Although the long term has shown that Martha was more capable of dealing with the stepfamily situation than the more idealistic Susan was, she was often considered the "wicked stepmother" because of her determination to establish rules, have privacy, and not be overrun by the family. Unlike Susan, Martha did not expect Frank's children to love her and she was not devastated when they showed hostility. The hope and the desire to create an instant bond, which are so often present in women as they meet and grow to know their future stepchildren, is simply not realistic. The stepmother is *not* their mother, and it is a rare relationship in life that is a loving one from the start.

If one piece of advice could be given to a woman who is dating a man with children, it would be, "Hold back." You will have plenty of time to get to know the children and to work out a long-term relationship if you marry. Be friendly and open to friendship, but let the child come to you. Generally it is better to be reserved than to be ebullient. Children are instinctively wise about how adults feel toward them, and they are usually more comfortable if they are given time and plenty of room before they are asked to make any kind of commitment.

If a child views you, rightly or wrongly, as the cause of his or her parents' separation, you should expect hostility. Excuses and explanations will probably do no good; you can only remain firm in your commitment to the child's father and assume that this relationship will have the strength to overcome hostility.

It is important to remember that although *when* you marry you agree to become a part of your husband's family, *before* you marry you should concentrate on your love relationship. It is the cornerstone upon which the stepfamily must be built.

A divorced woman who becomes a stepmother has often suffered a loss of self-esteem. She therefore wants this new relationship to work and is determined not to make the same mistakes again. She hopes to keep the love, even the romance, alive as long as possible and has convinced herself that everything will work out fine. Trying to attend to her love relationship and at the same time give time and attention to

her lover's children is an overwhelming objective from the
beginning. Ultimately, she is forming a permanent relationship
with a man, a relationship that will last beyond the time that
the stepchildren will live with the couple. The quality of the
time she spends with her future husband is crucial, for unless
they are able to form a strong, permanent bond, everyone will
suffer. As Emily B. and John S. Visher advise in their book
*Stepfamilies: A Guide to Working with Stepparents and
Stepchildren,*

> Parent-child relationships have preceded the
> new couple relationship. Because of this, many par-
> ents feel that it is a betrayal of the earlier parent-
> child bond to form a primary relationship with their
> new partner. A primary couple relationship, how-
> ever, is usually crucial for the continuing existence
> of the stepfamily, and therefore is very important for
> the children as well as for the adults. A strong adult
> bond can protect the children from another family
> loss, and it also can provide the children with a
> positive model for their own eventual marriage
> relationship. The adults often need to arrange time
> alone to help nourish this important couple
> relationship.[4]

It is often hard to find this necessary time alone, not only
because of the busy nature of our lives, but also because a
parent often feels guilty about the primacy of the love relationship over the parent-child relationship.

So the stepmother begins her journey heavily burdened
with emotional baggage. She is often perceived by her future
stepchildren as an intruder, as sexually wanton and destructive, and she is more often than not struggling with her own
sense of hurt self-esteem and loss. Add a dash of guilt because
she wants and needs to be alone with her lover and cannot
immediately like his children, and one wonders if it is worth all
the bother.

It is. Just remember that the children are most likely
going through their own emotional difficulties, and hold back.
Don't expect them to like you right away, and if they do, expect

them to change their minds. Concentrate on your love for their father and strengthen it so that when you stand together to exchange your marriage vows you can feel happy in the knowledge that your commitment is sincere and that you are willing to work together to find your stepfamily's particular path toward happiness.

3

The Wedding

JUST HOW MANY OF US
ARE GETTING MARRIED ANYWAY?

A FEW YEARS AGO I ATTENDED A PERFORMANCE OF BRAHMS'S *REQUIEM,* and when the chorale finished the last note and walked from the stage, the woman behind me sighed, "Now I *really* feel dead."

Like the woman behind me at the concert, when we were proclaimed man and wife, I turned to Lee and said, "Now I *really* feel married."

When Lee and I stood before a justice of the peace with our son, Adam, in my arms, we had been married three times.

Our first marriage was a personal commitment we made when we moved in together in 1965. As far as we were concerned, this was our true marriage. After living together for almost a year we went to Mexico, where Lee obtained a unilateral divorce and we married. The Mexican divorce and marriage presented a curious and annoying tangle of legalities that took over two years to settle. In 1968, our attorney advised us to marry again in the United States, and by this time Adam was a year old.

The three of us traveled to Connecticut where we obtained a marriage license and appeared before a justice of the peace. We introduced ourselves as Karen Savage and Lee Savage, and as we stood there together in the room, Adam squirming in my arms, the justice asked, "Do you want the traditional marriage ceremony, or shall I just pronounce you man and wife?"

"Just pronounce us man and wife," we answered in unison, and that, finally, was that.

Looking back, the most frustrating aspect of our marriage was not the legal hassles or the time it took, but rather the fact that we were unable to celebrate it with friends and family. We also had no practical opportunity to include our children in our marriage ceremony. By the time we were married by the justice of the peace, we thought of it as no more than a legal necessity, like putting an official seal on a completed document.

It was unfortunate, however. A wedding is a life ceremony, an important marking in one's life. It is a celebration based on a series of traditions that have developed over the years. Although the various symbols in the ceremony have outlasted the social customs on which they were based, a marriage nevertheless remains one of the most important celebrations in our society.

The fact that one marriage out of three ends in divorce, or that one marriage out of five is a second marriage, does not alter the basic intent of a public commitment to the idea of matrimony. Even that paragon of contemporary good behavior, Miss Manners, says, "Traditional ceremonies, whether civil or religious, express hopes and ideals; they do not make realistic predictions."[1]

Marriages are family affairs, and traditionally the bride's family was most involved with the ceremony itself. The mother of the bride was expected to make most of the arrangements, and the father of the bride "gave his daughter away."

This type of family involvement is not expected in a second marriage. A woman who is marrying again usually wants to organize her own wedding, and to be "given away" by a father not once but twice seems slightly absurd.

A marriage is still a family affair, however, except this

time the family usually includes the bride and groom's children. If a traditional first marriage represented a young girl leaving her family to join in marriage with a man, a second marriage represents two people not so much leaving a family as entering one.

It is interesting to read the marriage vows, which are basically the same whether one is marrying for the first or the fifth time. Two people pledge their troth, or fidelity, in love and honor, duty and service, and faith and tenderness. They agree to live together, cherish one another, and be loving and faithful through plenty or want, joy or sorrow, sickness or health, as long as they both shall live.

The vows that a couple make to each other are the primary vows of the marriage. In the Catholic Church, the marriage ceremony is a sacrament administered by a man and woman to each other. The bond that is vowed between them is the key to the stability of the families that are also being united. It is important to remember this, not only in planning a wedding but in setting up the long-term relationships between the various individuals involved. Unless a stepfamily is based upon a firm commitment to the marriage itself, it is unlikely that it can survive.

There are, however, far-reaching implications to these vows when one or both of the two people speaking are already parents. The vows imply a mutual commitment between two adults, and by joining themselves together, a parent or parents make a public commitment to join their families as well. If you change the words slightly in the first vow of the marriage ceremony, it reads as follows:

"Wilt thou have this family to be thy family, and wilt thou pledge thy troth to them, in all love and honor, in all duty and service, in all faith and tenderness, to live with them, and cherish them, according to the ordinance of God, in the holy bond of family?"

Regardless of whether or not the children are expected to live with their parents, these marriage vows should be considered carefully. A child is an integral part of his or her parent and will remain so as long as they both shall live. It is important to remember this when marrying a parent.

One of the most often repeated laments I hear in working with stepmothers is, "But I thought I was marrying *him*, not his children!" This notion, which invariably proves to be false, is often reflected in the marriage ceremony. Nancy, who ended up having her three stepchildren live with her, recalls, "It never occurred to me to include the children in our wedding . . . because it never occurred to me that they would become a part of our life together. As far as I was concerned, I was simply in love . . . and happier than I had ever been before. Dick's children lived with their mother in another city, and I didn't even expect to see them very often. I thought of the wedding as Dick's and my wedding, *our* day, the official beginning of our life together. Little did I know. . . ."

Ten years later, this woman looks back and sees that she was as naive about what marriage held in store for her as the most sheltered blushing bride in Victorian society, even though she was forty-one, divorced, and with a teenage son of her own. Nancy, like so many women marrying again, was filled with hope and romantic expectations. She had finally ended a long and unhappy marriage and had met Dick, who loved her in a way she had not known before. She was convinced that their love would make everything work out, and she planned her wedding day in a euphoric cloud, without once thinking about her specific responsibility or relationship to his three children. She admits she exchanged vows without even thinking about the real meaning of her promise.

By pledging her love and honor to Dick, Nancy agreed to help him shoulder his responsibilities. These responsibilities turned out to be his children, who were brought to her for care when their biological mother became too ill to care for them. Her pledge to be his loving and faithful wife meant leaving her job and her apartment and returning to the aisles of the supermarket in order to make a home for her husband's children. She was not legally bound to change her life for these children, but she felt morally bound by her marriage vows to Dick.

Not only will the bride and groom's marriage be affected by the children involved, the children themselves will be greatly affected by the marriage. Whether or not the children involved are pleased about their parents' marriage, it is usually a fact that is beyond their control. For many children, the marriage will have a major impact on their lives. It will determine who they spend their family time with, who will have power in their lives, and whom they will be expected to love, or to show love towards.

This does not mean that you should ask the children's permission to marry. This decision is between the two people who plan to live together long after the children have left home, and although the children's needs must be carefully considered, the final decision rests with the adult couple. They also accept the responsibility of creating a family, and it seems only fair that they themselves should be the primary ones to vow fidelity to the family bond.

The bride and groom should determine how the marriage will be celebrated and should not lose sight of the fact that it is *their* wedding. Nevertheless, the most important thing to remember in a subsequent marriage ceremony is the children involved. Again Miss Manners comments, "The close relatives whose cooperation adult bridal couples most need are their children. If anyone is to be given a role in the ceremony, it should be they."[2]

When a couple who have children marry, the ceremony should reflect that families are getting married, and the children should be given the opportunity to participate in things like planning the wedding—in choosing clothes, food, music, decorations, and sometimes even the vows that will be exchanged.

Young children are often excited by the prospect of a marriage and are usually willing to think of their parents' marriage as including them. A young girl of four, who had not known her biological father, was thrilled when her mother married a man she had been dating.

"Me and Mama and Bill got married!" she proudly announced to her Sunday School class.

Older children may be more reluctant to be included in the ceremony, but they should be asked. If they choose not to participate, their wish should be respected. The bride and groom should also adhere to their own personal desires for their wedding and should not allow the whims of others to infringe upon their day.

There are various possibilities for including children in a wedding. The most common is for the children to serve as ushers or bridesmaids. A son can serve as his father's best man. A woman's children can accompany her as she enters and stand with her during the ceremony. Some families have written vows to be exchanged between the groom and his stepchildren or between the bride and her stepchildren. The important thing to remember is that even though families are being united, these families are represented, at least as far as the wedding ceremony is concerned, by the bride and groom, and their sense of propriety and good taste is of the utmost importance.

Everyone looks forward to their marriage as a time of joy, to be shared with those they love. To have someone at a wedding who is not only not joyful but also angry or unhappy can be a blight on a happy event. Since stepfamilies come into being after a loss, however, there may be individuals in attendance who cast a pall over the festivities. It could be a former in-law, or a grandparent, but as often as not it is one of the children. One mother tells of hearing her daughters sobbing behind her in the church as she spoke her vows.

Be prepared for some who may not share the joy of your wedding day. Your marriage makes fact what had been only a possibility before, the children who continue to nurture hope that their biological parents will reunite, or who want their parent to remain single, must come to terms with reality. Even if they do not want you as a stepmother, after the wedding you are one, and the ceremony puts a period on that fact. Be happy with those who are happy also and concentrate on sharing your joy rather than trying to give condolence or show irritation. Think of the day as your celebration and as a way to make a statement of hope and faith in the future.

If you feel positively about your wedding and know how you wish it to be celebrated, it will most likely be satisfying for your family and friends. Whether the wedding is extraordinary or quiet, it is the attitude of the marrying couple that will set the tone for the event.

Irina, who had never been married, met William, who had recently been widowed. He had three teenage children whose religious upbringing had been guided primarily by their mother, who was a conservative Episcopalian. Elaborate rituals and expressive shows of affection or emotion were quite foreign to the children. Irina, however, was born in Russia and had come to America as a child after living in displaced-persons camps in Europe. She had grown up in a closely knit community of refugees, many of whom had never learned to speak English. When Irina and William decided to marry, the children were pleased, but they wondered how they would feel about an elaborate wedding conducted in a foreign language. Irina knew exactly what she wanted, however, and the wedding took place at a Russian Orthodox church that had served the Russian émigré community for years.

The wedding was different from anything William's children had experienced. For them it was interesting, even exotic. As far as Irina was concerned it was representative of herself and her family history, and she wanted her wedding to be a statement of all these things. She also wanted the wedding to bring her future stepchildren into this circle, to encourage them to accept her and what she was. She saw the wedding as symbolic of growth, of enlarging both her and her future family's life. She did not want to compete with what they had had with their own mother but wanted to start something new with them: a new set of rituals, new ways of being together, new ways of expression.

The wedding did include the children. Irina's future stepdaughter was the maid of honor, and the two sons were ushers and stood with their father. The wedding was conducted in Old Church Slavonic, the language used in the liturgy of the Russian Orthodox Church, with the priest occasionally rendering a phrase in English. Although the children obviously did

not understand everything that the priest said, they participated fully. It was the spirit of the wedding that counted. It
was a wedding that expressed commitment and enthusiasm for
a family life together.

Little needs to be said about the honeymoon trip except
that it should include only the honeymooners. Sometimes
couples think they could or should take the children for a
family trip, but a honeymoon is not the time for that. It is
important to establish the privacy of the couple right away,
even if only a short trip is possible. Traditionally the honeymoon was for the private consummation of the marriage vows,
and in a marriage with existing children, it is probably even
more important for the couple to go away privately than it is
for a couple marrying for the first time. One must remember
that unless the couple survives the family will not survive, and
attention and time must be allowed for the couple to be alone
together. It is better to establish this precedent right away
than to hope that somehow it will happen as time goes on. It
won't. Take your honeymoon while you can, because when you
return home to your family, you'll find that the honeymoon is
over soon enough.

4

Coming Home

DURING A RECENT CONFERENCE ON STEPFAMILIES, A PANEL OF THREE teenage stepchildren spoke of their experiences. When asked what their primary goals in life were, the two females responded, "a career," and the only male, Peter, said "marriage and family."

"What do you think of when you say marriage and family?" he was asked.

"Well, I guess I mean mostly family. A big family. Lots of brothers and sisters to grow up together, do things together. A real home."

"Would you consider your stepfamily such a family, since there are a total of six children?"

"Oh no, not really. You see, my stepsisters are spoiled by their mother. She was an only child and, well, just raised her daughters differently. My own mother, on the other hand, was one of eleven children. She had a wonderful home, the kids were real close. They still do things together a lot and talk about how great their home was."

44

Peter's view of family says a lot. His yearning for home and family is touching and is also indicative of our collective fantasy about home. It is the home that his mother has described to him from her childhood memories, and that she remembers as a warm, loving, and supportive place. It is not, however, a home that he has actually experienced. Although his stepfamily fits his description of a happy home—lots of children growing up together, doing things together—the reality of his home life just doesn't match up to his fantasy.

"There's no place like home," the old song says, and the contemporary musicians Simon and Garfunkel sing poignantly, ".... Homeward bound, I wish I was.... Home....," while John Denver calls, "Country roads ... take me home. ..."

We like to think of home as a place where you are comforted, where you feel safe and can find respite from the aggressiveness of the outside world. It's where you belong, where you can lick your wounds, where you can find sympathy, good food, and a comfortable bed. The fact that this is often not the reality does not diminish the ideal that we hold when we think of home.

Although the concept of home is often romanticized with the cozy houses pictured on Christmas cards, or with images of rose-covered cottages back in the old country, it is also a concept fixed firmly in our psyches.

Robert Frost wrote, in "The Death of the Hired Man,"

Home is the place where, when you have to go there,
They have to take you in.
I should have called it
Something you somehow haven't to deserve.

Here Frost hits on perhaps the key to our idea of home—it's a place you don't have to "deserve." You belong there, it's where you're from, it's your place on the earth and a place you can always go back to. One of the best known parables of the

New Testament is the parable of the prodigal son, who, when "he would fain have filled his belly with the husks that the swine did eat: and no man gave unto him. . . . And he arose, and came to his father." When he had no place else to go, in other words, he returned home.

In her study on the future of marriage, Jessie Bernard states,

> The concept of a "home" [is that] which can serve as a firm, permanent, solid, stable base from which one can sally forth, confident that there is a secure place to return to. . . . In a world of increasing mobility and flux, the need for such an anchored base becomes even greater than in the past. The individual can tolerate a great deal of rootless movement if he knows that there is a place to return to. Until now the family home has provided this base. The prodigal son knew that he could return.[1]

This concept of home, however, is based on a primary bond of our society, that of "kinship." As the folk saying goes, "Blood's thicker than water," and according to Bernard, the concept of kinship is one of the most powerful ever created by the human imagination. "It has [been] recognized for centuries," she states, "that 'kinfolk' do not necessarily love or even like one another; . . . but the psychological function served by kinship—that of supplying an unassailable and indestructible tie with a group of people who had no choice but to accept you—remains."[2]

When two people marry they implicitly agree to form a home together, and most women would love to make a home that is all the songs and poems imply: warm, comforting, a safe and nurturing place. When a woman marries a father, however, the home she will work to create cannot help but fall short of the traditional concept of home, because her home is not where her stepchildren originated, and she is not "blood kin" to them.

Since the stepmother is not related by blood to her

stepchildren, the bonding that is so intrinsic to the concept of home does not automatically exist. Basic to the relationship between stepmother and stepchild is the knowledge of both that they are not "kin."

Nevertheless, the children are kin to their father, and his need to be with and to parent his children must be addressed. When a woman marries a father the home that the two of them create will almost always include his children in one way or another. As one stepmother who was interviewed said, "If you love your husband then you must make his children feel welcome in your home. Otherwise he loses them and that's not fair to him. It's one of the most important ways you can show your love for him."

The children, however, often have trouble with this new home. They may not have their own room and the house may seem strange to them. They may be uncertain about what to call their father's wife or her children or her parents. Initially there is nothing "familiar" in this new "family."

Instead of "going home," the children have entered a strange land where they cannot be sure what is expected of them. Do they have to make the bed or does it matter? Can they drink Coke in the living room or is it forbidden? The essence of our concept of home is that which is familiar, comfortable, and predictable. Usually, none of these things initially exist in a stepmother's home.

The home, therefore, that the stepmother is expected to create is actually a new concept. It cannot be based on a collective fantasy of home. There are no songs or poems about going back home to that dear ol' stepmother of mine.

There are no fixed rules for making a stepfamily home, but it is helpful to think of the concept of "home" as different from that of "house," and of "homemaker" as different from "house-keeper."

A housekeeper can be hired and fired and is expected to perform particular household tasks. A homemaker, on the other hand, creates a home from her own individual perception of what a home should be. Creating a home is one of the most important tasks of a stepmother, and in trying to decide the home she wants to make she needs to consider three factors equally: the father of her stepchildren, the children themselves, and herself.

My husband and I made several attempts at creating a home before we found something that worked. To begin with, we found an apartment in Greenwich Village which had enough space for my two children as well as for his children to have their own bedrooms when they visited.

On Saturday mornings we would pick up Lee's children, who lived in rural Rockland County, and bring them down for the weekend in the city. Lee and I were both working, which meant that on Saturdays we had errands to do: laundry to be taken out, dry cleaning picked up, groceries purchased, and all the other jobs that had been put off during the week. At the same time we needed to be sure that the children were being taken care of or in some way entertained.

One would assume that entertaining children in New York City would have been a cinch, but the reverse was true. The boys were not used to being in the city and were still too young to be allowed to roam by themselves. It was necessary for them to stay in the apartment unless we were able to accompany them. It didn't take long for them to resent being brought into New York, where they had to sit around inside while their father and stepmother did errands.

In order to make their weekends more pleasant we took regular trips to Central Park, the skating rink, the zoo, and all the museums. As we walked with our combined families past yet another vendor selling something that one of our children insisted on having, we found we could easily spot other divorced fathers with their children. They too were overly solicitous, and the children were always burdened down with balloons, candy, or stuffed animals as they whined and begged for more. The fathers all had a look we called *dépaysé*—taken out of their own country. Everyone looked out of place, the children with too many things that they had demanded and the parents trying to exorcise guilt or attain affection by meeting the children's demands.

These exhausting weekends didn't work. Although Lee's

daughter Kate was young and loved being with her stepsister, the boys complained bitterly. They were bored, they felt hemmed in, and they hated it. They were, after all, at an age when their friends and social activities were very important. There were plenty of community activities for them at home— Little League, boy scouts, or just neighborhood buddies— which they missed when they came into the city. It was evident that Pete and Willy never attached themselves to their room. They made no attempt to decorate it, to put up pictures or ask for special curtains or bedspreads. Clearly their attitude about our apartment in New York City was that it was "*not* a nice place to visit, and we don't want to live there."

I often felt that it would just be easier on all of us if they didn't come in at all and Lee visited them instead. For Lee, however, this was not an alternative. After living with his children for over twelve years he did not want to have their time together reduced to a Sunday afternoon riding around in Rockland County looking for something to do. Family life is built on day-in, day-out living together, not short visits with strained attempts at making conversation and catching up on school activities. Lee had been a part of his children's daily life and now he was beginning to feel superfluous; he did not belong to their house anymore, or even to their community.

From the boys' perspective, their old day-to-day life of having Dad around almost all the time had been greatly altered. Their father no longer lived in their home. That was the reality, and it was very hard for them to find another place where it was comfortable for them to be together.

Although the boys' insistence that they hated to visit us because we lived in the city might only have been a cover for their anger at our marriage, we decided to get a house in the country so we could all spend time in a place that did not primarily "belong" more to my children than to Lee's. It was, as it were, neutral territory. The country house also fulfilled our rather romantic notions about "home": a big yard, woods nearby, a big kitchen that I hoped soon to fill with the smell of gingerbread and cookies baking. We would no longer feel cast adrift among the seeming multitude of divorced parents spending an anxious day in the park with their children.

Actually, this solution did work much better for us. The boys had ample space to play, they could take off for the woods and stay gone for hours without our worrying. They could be alone if they wished, and the house was big enough for all of us to be together without bumping into each other constantly.

This solution worked for a while, but circumstances eventually forced us to sell the country house, leave the city, and buy a home in the suburbs. As we tried different living arrangements, one factor was always key: there would always be a place for Lee's children in our home. This was very important for us. Until they became adults with their own residences, we wanted them to feel they had a special place with us.

The needs of visiting stepchildren are important, and in a society in which living space is at a greater premium than in the past, making arrangements for them can be a real challenge. Twenty years ago such things as a large city apartment, a country house, or an ample suburban home were possible. Today, however, most stepfamilies find themselves in much more crowded circumstances. It is often difficult to give visiting stepchildren much privacy, and wide open spaces where they can wander and play undisturbed are rare.

Many families cannot allocate separate bedrooms for visiting children. Often they must double up with the children who are living in the home. Not only does this often cause the visiting child to feel like an outsider, it can also infringe on the children at home. They are asked to share toys, bedroom, time, and even friends with someone they have not chosen. As Linda Bird Francke says in her book *Growing Up Divorced*, these "family groups are created out of marriage licenses rather than blood and shared history."[3]

Although stepchildren may initially visit primarily to be with their father, eventually arrangements must be made to accommodate the family as a whole: the visiting children, live-in children, and parents. Each family has to work on these arrangements according to its own particular circumstances, which will differ from family to family.

When a family is trying to work out its own best solution it is helpful to remember that a stepfamily is not a biological family and the same rules simply do not apply. In fact, there *are* no rules, because we do not yet have established traditions or societal rules for stepfamilies. Most often what is true for a biological family is *not* true for a stepfamily.

Another reality in most stepfamilies is that whatever arrangements you make will probably have to be rethought and rearranged a number of times during your stepfamily life. More than biological families, stepfamilies seem to need to try different ways of living together. This means that a stepmother must work to be flexible.

One stepmother recognized, just in time, that her inflexibility jeopardized her marriage. In the previous chapter on weddings, Nancy realized only after she spoke her vows that her marriage would include Dick's three children. During their first year together, when they were living in an apartment in New York and both had full-time jobs, they received a late-night phone call. Dick's ex-wife was in the hospital and would need extended care. Six hours later, three teenage children, whom Nancy had seen only occasionally, came to stay.

It was clear that their life had been chaotic. Their poor diet was reflected in their complexions, their clothes were outgrown and dingy, and their personal hygiene was casual at best. Nancy was struck by their obvious need to be cared for and she and Dick immediately made arrangements to sell their apartment and buy a house in the suburbs. Nancy quit her job to make a home for these children.

Nancy was by nature a fastidious woman who liked her life organized and everything clean and neat. Dick was a casual housekeeper but when only the two of them were living together Nancy could joke about his habits. She teased him about how he wasn't happy unless he had something *growing* in the refrigerator. He was only one person, however, and when

his children arrived Nancy immediately found that life with
one disorderly person was very different from life with three
messy, disgruntled teenagers who resented every suggestion
she made.

They left clothes, books, and empty plates all over the
house. They had no interest in keeping their rooms neat and
wore their clothes rumpled or dirty. Their table manners were
atrocious and while one seemed to spend hours every morning
and night in the shower, another refused to bathe at all. Nancy
felt not only angry but threatened. They had just moved into
a new community and she did not want *her* stepchildren
walking around their new neighborhood looking like waifs. She
found herself shouting to Dick, "If they're going to live in *my*
house and *my* town, they're going to be like me!" She found she
resented Dick more and more because he refused to discipline
them. She felt that the entire responsibility of turning these
sloppy children into civilized young adults fell on her shoul-
ders.

Nancy was a recovered alcoholic and had participated in
Alcoholics Anonymous before she married Dick. She found
herself wanting an escape, and recognizing the danger signals
she started attending AA meetings again. At the first meeting
she found herself talking about her stepchildren and how
impossible her life had become. She almost couldn't stop
talking—it was as if the floodgates of anger and frustration
had finally been let open.

After the meeting another member of the group suggested
they go for a cup of coffee. She said that she understood exactly
what Nancy was going through.

As they sat over their coffee the woman looked at Nancy
directly and said, "If you don't stop hating his children, your
husband is going to stop loving you. I know, because that's
exactly what happened to me."

This woman's words hit home. Nancy realized that her
attitude was destructive for the family as a whole. She knew
also that she couldn't change overnight and she couldn't do
it alone. By returning to AA and talking out her problems
with a supportive group, she began to find a way to work out

her stepfamily relationships. It wasn't easy but the advice and support she received from AA made all the difference.

"Take it one day at a time," "What you resist persists," "Change yourself, not others." This advice, familiar to those who participate in AA, helped Nancy make a home for her stepfamily. She learned to let go, step back a bit, and stop trying to make her stepchildren over in her own image. AA encouraged her to "reconnect" herself to a higher power, stop feeling like a failure, and simply do the best she could. It occurred to Nancy that the traditional homilies about "Home sweet home" and "There's no place like home" were replaced in her mind with the more realistic attitude expressed in AA.

In talking with her AA group Nancy realized that the one thing that bothered her the most about her stepchildren was their table manners. She let everything else go but insisted that they come to meals clean and that the family have quiet, civil dinners together. A small demand, but nevertheless one that set a precedent for how the family would relate to one another, and it helped her feel comfortable during one very important family activity.

The children did improve as they lived with her. Their personal habits, their grades, and even their relationships with their peers were noticeably better. There were few thank-yous, however, because children rarely thank parents for discipline and care. In the following years two of the children chose to return to their mother, and Nancy's stepdaughter left to go away to boarding school.

Initially this was a blow to Nancy. After all she had done for them! She bit her tongue, however, and saved her anger for her AA meetings. The group had enough distance to remind her that no matter what had happened, the children's mother was their natural mother, and they *needed* to go back to her before they could break away and become adults. The group also reminded Nancy that she had done all she could, and that she could now look forward to some time alone with her husband.

No sooner had she adjusted to the empty house, however,

than her college-age stepchildren decided to spend summers there. When this proved difficult Nancy turned the house over to them and spent her summers in a vacation house two hours away. She and Dick were together for weekends but spent their weeks apart.

This solution would seem strange in a biological family but in this stepfamily it worked. The children loved being with their father. Nancy had turned her house over to a group of very casual housekeepers, but she felt it was necessary for a period of time. As the years have progressed, the family has found that time spent together has become more pleasant than they had ever expected. Two of Nancy's stepchildren moved back in with her after college graduation, and as adults they have worked out a very satisfying family relationship.

Nancy's experience points out that flexibility is very important for the family. Making a stepfamily home is a constant, ongoing, changing endeavor. Some of the problems are never solved, and no solutions are permanent. With stepfamilies nothing is ever "fixed." The stepfamily home redefines itself constantly.

Another couple I know also found that the best solution to combining two families was not to combine them. The wife lives in her own house and the husband in his, each with their own teenage children. They spend weekends together and look forward to the day when both nests will be empty and they can move in together.

The point is not whether stepfamilies can or cannot live together, but rather that each stepfamily must look at its own situation and figure out what is actually best for it, even if it seems abnormal.

With stepfamilies there is no normal or abnormal. As Nancy stated, "Whatever works, you *do*." Stepfamilies are pioneers, finding a path through unmarked territory. To succeed as a stepfamily there must be a willingness to experiment, to try unusual alternatives, to step back from the "norm" and resist unrealistic goals.

Although the needs of the father and the family unit are important, they are no more important than the needs of the stepmother. A stepmother who grows to feel that she is no more than a housekeeper can grow angry and bitter. I remember how I grew to resent the overwhelming demands of a combined family. The Friday- and Sunday-evening routine was enough to try the patience of a saint: packing up children, groceries, and clothes in the city, driving to Rockland County to pick up Lee's children, and then proceeding to Connecticut with five children, all of them tired and needing to go to the bathroom frequently, sometimes fighting, sometimes falling into sleep. I felt as if we were a traveling band of gypsies.

At the time, I often felt that I was the one bearing the brunt of trying to coordinate this family: the meals, the laundry, the activities, the discipline, the traveling. The duties seemed endless. I totally agreed with Montaigne's remark, "There is scarcely any less bother in the running of a family than in that of an entire state."

If I were running a state, however, I would at least have been compensated with a nice title and salary. Running this family made me feel primarily like a housekeeper and maid. In my years working with stepfamilies I have found this complaint to be one of the most common. Even when a stepmother has her own profession and has no children of her own, she often feels that she spends her time taking care of her stepchildren when they are around.

Most men are relieved and pleased to have someone around to help them take care of their visiting children. Although many men agree, at least intellectually, that they should participate in the physical care of their children, it is often very easy to slip back into traditional roles. A stepmother does not need to make sweeping statements or ultimatums about what she will or will not do, but if her vision of a home and family includes the active participation of her husband, she should be able to expect his support. It has been my experience that the fathers who are most involved with their children, from changing diapers and cooking Sunday breakfast to giving driving lessons or helping with math homework, are the fathers who receive the most satisfying rewards from family life.

No matter how much a husband participates in the care and feeding of the family, however, much of the physical work that is necessary falls to the woman of the house, and, as a stepmother, she is performing this work for someone else's children.

Even the most committed stepmother can begin to doubt why she is cleaning, mending, cooking, and nurturing these children. No matter how important creating a home is, a stepmother needs some degree of separateness.

One stepmother started her married life with the full intention of taking care of every need, both physical and emotional, of her three young stepchildren, but she found that she eventually became resentful and angry. Pat met Dan shortly after his wife had left him, leaving behind three children under six years old. Pat was single with no children and was teaching and working on her doctorate. Before meeting Dan she had planned to finish her doctorate, buy a house, and make a home for foster children. She knew she had a great need to nurture and take care of others.

When Pat met Dan's children she could hardly wait to take them under her wing and mother them. They responded to her attention with such obvious affection that Pat felt she had found the greatest joy in life. During the wedding ceremony, when the minister asked "Who gives this woman to be wed?," Dan's five-year-old son solemnly announced, "I do!" His four-year-old brother followed with "I do, too," and the two-year-old chirped happily, "Me, too!"

Pat knew she had married a family. This pleased her, for this was what she had wanted. The children were young and had been abandoned by their mother. Even though she was shocked by the enormity of their needs as well as by the fact that she suddenly had *no* time to herself, she felt happy and fulfilled. Pat states: "I felt that they were *my* kids. I took them on with great joy. They called me 'Mommie' from the beginning. I *wanted* to 'do' for them, make a home. I wanted to bake cookies, read bedtime stories, take care of them, nurture them. I felt true love for these children and I enjoyed working for them. My motto is 'Work is love made visible.' "

Pat's primary image of the stepmother came from "Cinderella," and her aim was to redefine the term. She vowed always to love the children and never push them away, no matter how difficult it became. She wanted to help heal them.

After the initial excitement and euphoria family life settled into a more prosaic pattern. The children's mother returned to the community and arrangements were made for regular visits with her. The children switched from calling Pat "Mommie" to simply calling her "M." As time went on Pat began to wonder why *she* was the one always sewing on the missing button, or why the children returned from visits to their mother with bags of dirty clothes. The care and feeding of these young children took up all Pat's time, while their mother enjoyed the freedom of a single life.

When Pat became pregnant she was thrilled at the prospect of her own baby, but she was determined not to let the new child diminish her time with and commitment to the other children. The house was filled with excitement when she came home with her new son, and everyone wanted to help take care of him. Determined not to leave anyone out, Pat tried to include everyone in the care of the baby, as she also tried to pay equal attention to all. Suddenly she was overwhelmed with tasks. She became tense and had trouble nursing. The baby began to lose weight and had to be returned to the hospital.

Pat became furious that she was caring for someone else's three children while she was struggling just to feed her own. She heard herself saying "*your* children," and "*my* baby." "Cinderella's stepmother," she thought guiltily.

Pat found an unusual solution to her problem: she decided to finish her dissertation. This seemed crazy on the surface: what sense did it make for this woman to start back to work on her dissertation when she had four young children to care for?

It made sense because it gave her private time. Pat would never have gone up to her room with the baby and closed the door on her stepchildren, but she could be alone if she were working on her dissertation. No one's feelings were hurt. Pat needed this time, space, and privacy as well as a sense of something separate from the demands of her family.

Pat hired teenagers who came in after school to watch her stepchildren. She would go up to her bedroom, close the door, nurse and hold the baby, then read and organize her research. This gave her three hours a day to herself. She defended her dissertation when she was pregnant with her second child, and started teaching again as soon as he was old enough to attend nursery school.

Pat wanted to be a mother. She wanted to make a home. She thrilled to the challenge of nurturing and helping her young stepchildren. But in order to be a homemaker rather than just a housekeeper she needed her own separateness within the family.

This notion of housekeeper/homemaker is important for the stepmother. It is easy to become resentful, angry, and irritable if you think you do nothing but fulfill the physical needs of stepchildren. A housekeeper can be hired but a homemaker is committed to an idea. The homemaker establishes an attitude, an atmosphere, and a place that reflect the "maker's" hopes and intent, even if the reality falls short of expectations. To create a warm, secure home, you need to feel good about yourself first. A happy stepmother will make a happier home.

Both Nancy and Pat found that a kind of separateness enabled them to be better homemakers for their stepchildren. In spite of good intentions and moral commitment, they found that without a "separate space" they grew angry and resentful. Although a woman's place is not necessarily in the home, without her positive sense and commitment a home is no more than a house.

It is the stepmother who plays the primary role in establishing the atmosphere of her home. She is creating this home for herself, her husband, and the children of the family. Although everyone's needs are important, they should be considered equally.

A stepmother is guiding her family through uncharted territory, and therefore has the freedom to experiment and try unusual solutions. Together, the family needs to find out what works for it and then do it. Then, when that stops working, it needs to try something else and do that.

When the honeymoon is over, it's really over, but the changing, shifting relationships in the stepfamily home are only beginning.

5

Becoming a Family

ONE STEP AT A TIME

WITHIN THE HOME, THERE IS THE FAMILY. JUST AS THE CONCEPT OF home needs to be redefined in terms of the stepfamily, the term "family" takes on new and different connotations when it is a stepfamily. The mother's place in the family is pivotal, and although countless studies have been done on "mothering," the stepmother finds herself with little guidance. Her role in the stepfamily is made more difficult because of the traditionally negative image of stepmothers, and of the absence of traditions, guidelines, and societal rules bearing on their role.

Estimates of the number of American adults who live in stepfamilies were 25 million in 1980. Approximately 15 million children have stepparents, and according to the U.S. Census Bureau's analysis of data, an estimated thirteen hundred new stepfamilies with children under the age of eighteen are forming every day. If the projections from Census Bureau statistics hold steady to the end of the decade, there will be more single-parent families and stepfamilies than traditional families.

Although there have been stepfamilies as long as there have been families, the number of stepfamilies is a relatively new phenomenon. This increase of stepfamilies is occurring so quickly that society has not had time to establish traditions and guidelines for the stepfamily and has not even been able to find a language that can be used to describe this family unit.

The absence of a positive stepfamily tradition and the lack of adequate terms to describe the complexities of stepfamily life are issues with almost all stepmothers. Stepmothers I have counseled or interviewed often admitted that their initial image of a stepmother was of the wicked stepmother from the fairy tales. These women were anxious to dispel that image by becoming "supermom"—loving, nuturing, and unselfish toward their stepchildren. When they could not be the all-loving supermom, they began to feel that they were the wicked stepmother after all.

Almost all contemporary literature on stepfamilies gives attention to fairy tales, probably because fairy tales are the oldest and best-known descriptions of step-relationships. If there is a collective image of stepmothers and stepchildren in our society, it is usually based on these unrealistic but symbolic tales. Because fairy tales have been a part of our culture for so many years, it is worthwhile to examine why they are so important to us all.

Bruno Bettelheim, in his fascinating study of fairy tales, *The Uses of Enchantment*, maintains that "the unrealistic nature of the tales . . . is an important device, because it makes obvious that the fairy tales' concern is not useful information about the external world, but the inner processes taking place in an individual."[1]

Although Bettelheim concentrates on the importance of fairy tales for children, he states that an individual returns to these stories over and over again, finding new meanings in them at different levels of psychological development.

These stories have survived for centuries because they do, in fact, contain certain truths to which we can all relate on some level. Although the "wicked stepmother" is the most obvious "step" image from the fairy tales, upon close reading other aspects of these stories emerge that show a striking parallel to what therapists are learning about the stressful circumstances of stepmothers.

"Snow White" is not only one of the best-known fairy tales, it is also particularly interesting for stepmothers because it contains the two images many of them have of their role. There is the negative image of the wicked stepmother who is insanely jealous of her stepdaughter and the image of Snow White herself, who is a kind of stepmother—the consummate saintly care-giver as she moves in to care for the seven dwarfs. She cooks, makes the beds, washes, and sews in exchange for the loving gratitude of the seven little men.

Many stepmothers begin stepfamily life believing they "should" be like Snow White, they "should" love their stepchildren, they "should" be understanding of the children's troubles, they "should" create a new and harmonious family that is better than what the children had before. Some therapists refer to the "tyranny of the shoulds." When the "shoulds" become overpowering, the stepmother experiences confusion, anger, and shame. She begins to feel like the wicked stepmother and recognizes strong negative feelings toward her stepchildren.

Emily and John Visher, pioneers in stepfamily therapy, clearly state that two of the most destructive myths a stepmother must deal with are the wicked-stepmother myth and the myth of instant love, which are both present in "Snow White." It is interesting to note that not only is the wicked stepmother vanquished in the story but Snow White leaves her role as mother to the dwarfs in order to marry the prince. She is not "complete" remaining in the forest, being only a nurturer and care-giver. The image of "saintly stepmother" and "wicked stepmother" are both left behind before Snow White can "live happily ever after."

Bettelheim maintains that fairy tales are valuable to children because they get across to the child that "a struggle against severe difficulties in life is unavoidable, is an intrinsic part of human existence—but that if one does not shy away, but steadfastly meets unexpected and often unjust hardships, one masters all obstacles and emerges victorious."[2]

Another aspect of fairy tales is that they consistently use images of trials to be met, journeys to be taken, goals to be achieved—i.e., they are procedural, moving from stage to stage until there is a final resolution. In this sense the imagery of many fairy tales is applicable to the process of becoming a stepfamily. When a stepfamily is formed it is, in a sense, at the beginning of a long journey or process.

Most of the guideposts are inadequate, however, and are based on society's concept of biological families. A stepfamily is not a biological family; where a biological family is a fact of blood relationships, each stepfamily must define itself. Our society has not had time to provide the rules, rituals, or support systems that are such a vital part of the biological family's sense of identity.

Since the fairy tale legacy has put such negative connotations on the word "step," attempts have been made to move away from the use of the term. "Combination families," "blended families," "reconstituted families," and "remarried" or "rem" families are terms used by therapists and laypeople. The parents' relationship in a stepfamily has been referred to as the "primary love relationship," and they are the "coparenting team" who are "recoupling." Books discuss "living in step," "stepping in," creative divorce, rewedded bliss, and the "second time around." This positive approach is undermined, however, with terms referring to the biological family as the normal, natural, intact, or unbroken family. Children in stepfamilies are from "broken homes," and biological parents are referred to as the "natural" or "real" parent. None of these terms quite fit, and as stepfamilies continue to emerge and find identity in our society the language will change and adjust itself to these new realities.

Like stepmothers, contemporary family therapists are finding that in treating the stepfamily they must deal with traditional negative connotations and at the same time work to develop new concepts in family therapy. Just as the terminology for step-relationships is still new and emerging, the understanding of the complexity of family-relationships is still in its early developmental stages. Family therapists who spend

their professional lives working with families and their problems are finding that there is a great need for clinical research
and data in this field. Many of the patterns found in stepfamily
relationships that would be indicative of deep trouble in a
biological family are normal for a stepfamily working toward
cohesion.

One particularly helpful study on stepfamilies was done
in 1980 by Dr. Patricia Lee Papernow, who wrote her doctoral
dissertation on the developmental stages of becoming a
stepparent.[3] Taking a Gestalt and "family systems" approach,
Papernow makes a convincing argument that an integrated
stepfamily evolves over a period of time and that this evolution
can be measured in a series of developmental stages.

Basic to Papernow's thesis is the family systems theory,
which views the family as a system in which all family
members are interdependent. The behavior of one member
affects all other members and is also a response to the behavior
of other family members. In their book *Ourselves and Our
Children,* the Boston Women's Health Book Collective use the
image of the body to describe the family systems method of
viewing the family:

> An analogy can be made to the human body, a
> system composed of organs, muscles, tissues, nerves,
> bones, fluids. All parts of the body are interconnected
> to compose a whole being. We can identify separate
> elements—a heart or specific muscles for instance—
> but no part exists in isolation. Our bodies are in
> constant motion—taking in air, digesting food, heal-
> ing themselves—and are routinely negotiating ex-
> changes between the inner environment and the
> outside world. Just as our bodies function because of
> the interrelationships of the different parts and the
> exchanges with the outside, so do our families.[4]

Although the family systems method is helpful in understanding stepfamilies, Papernow maintains that a "healthy"
biological family is not the same as a "healthy" stepfamily. She
summarizes the three characteristics of a "healthy" biological

family as defined by family theorists. First, healthy families have clear boundaries. This means that there are "intergenerational" boundaries between the adult couple and the children, and between the adult couple and their original family. Secondly, the family must have a "strong spouse subsystem," which means that the adult couple must have a "psychosocial territory of their own—a haven in which they can give each other emotional support." Thirdly, family systems theorists recognize a system of triangles that are formed among family members. In a triangle, two people become closer to each other while distancing a third person. These triangles are not in themselves unhealthy—for example, when a mother is sympathetic to a child after a father is unreasonable, or a brother takes up for his sister when she is late for dinner—as long as they are in motion, the makeup of the triangle shifting among family members. A triangle relationship is unhealthy when it is always the same two-against-one situation, with the insiders and the outsider remaining the same.

In a stepfamily, however, these characteristics cannot be expected to emerge for a long period of time. In new stepfamilies, for instance, there are no clear boundaries. Strong intergenerational bonds can be stronger than generational bonds. In other words, in the beginning of the marriage a parent often has a stronger bond with his or her biological child than with the spouse. Single parents have usually developed a closeness with their children, and no matter how loving and trusting they are of their new spouse, it takes time before the new parent is allowed "in" to that relationship.

It is also much more difficult for stepparents to form boundaries with their original family, the "ex-family," which can include ex-spouse, ex-spouse's new mate, ex-grandparents -uncles and -aunts, etc. Since these people are often directly related and involved with the child, the parent cannot be totally separate. Taking into account the addition of a new spouse's relatives and a new spouse's ex-spouse, and so on, the number of people involved in a stepfamily can climb very high. If one takes a "typical" family of two parents, two children, and four grandparents, and then divorces and remarries the parents to like families, the extended family number immediately goes from eight to twenty-four. In a stepfamily, therefore, there are simply more family members to deal with and the boundaries between these family members are often unclear.

This combination of strong bonds between parent and child, plus the high number of individuals outside the stepfamily who are in some way involved with it, make it difficult for the step-couple to find the "psychosocial territory of their own" that Papernow considers essential for a healthy biological family.

Thirdly, the fluctuating triangular relationships that exist in biological families can be rigid and fixed in a stepfamily, at least initially. For instance, the children may form a bond that excludes their stepparent, or a parent and biological child may form a bond excluding the new parent.

In other words, these red flags of warning in biological families can be considered the *norm* for stepfamilies. Stepfamilies' notion of a healthy family, as well as therapists' notions of how a healthy family functions, need to be changed to accommodate the stepfamily.

A good example of the traditional view of family therapy is the theory that if there is one family member who is a "problem," it is most likely a visible response to a deeper problem or "dysfunction" in the family itself. When this phenomenon is taken to extremes, one member can even be chosen as a "scapegoat." In her book *Surviving Family Life,* Dr. Sonya Rhodes states,

> [The family] enter therapy because one of the children is creating a disaster in the family. This can be anything from disobedience to drug abuse, sexual promiscuity, or running away from home. The family is at a loss to explain the child's explosive behavior and usually believes he has "turned bad." In fact, a disturbed adolescent is revealing the stress in the family. His or her behavior acts as a pressure valve to release tension that is building up somewhere in the family.

She goes on to say,

> Psychiatric problems for any member of the family at this stage signal a wider illness in the family as a whole. Sometimes one member of the family is elected to be "sick" and is scapegoated by the family. The unhappy relationships of all the members of the family are filtered through this one disturbed person.[5]

Although this theory makes sense in a biological family, the troubled child in a stepfamily may simply be working through his or her sense of loss and conflicting loyalties, which is an expected and normal process in a stepfamily.

In spite of the differences between biological families and stepfamilies, the use of the family systems theory of viewing the stepfamily as a changing living system, in which all parts are interdependent, helps to bring certain aspects of stepparenting into clearer focus. Since by definition stepfamilies are born of loss, the stepmother almost always become a part, at least initially, of a frail, injured system that is trying to recover. To return to the image of the body to represent a family, a new stepfamily is like a body that is in the process of healing. Even after it heals, there will be scars. A part of that healing will be both rejection and adjustment. Parts of the system may be much more vulnerable and in need of attention. The overall goal is for that system to become unified and healthy.

To achieve these goals, according to Papernow, the stepfamily must move through a series of stages. Although the marriage certificate legally creates an instant stepfamily, the real family is a long time in the making. In her longitudinal research of nine stepparents, Papernow has designated a "Stepfamily Cycle" based on the Gestalt "experience cycle." She theorizes that stepfamilies go through recognizable stages of development. Like the stages in the Gestalt cycle these can be used to define the point at which help is needed, to define what will facilitate movement to the next phase, and ultimately to guide the family toward a sense of completion and satisfaction.

Papernow defines the Stepfamily Cycle as having seven stages. First is the fantasy stage, in which stepparents have positive fantasies about parenting their mates' children. They expect to love and nurture their stepchildren, or perhaps to help "heal" their loss.

Second is the assimilation or "immersion," stage, in which stepparents experience a period of considerable confusion, anxiety, and disorientation because of unexpectedly negative feelings of jealousy, resentment, shame, and self-blame. At this stage a stepmother may feel "outside" the parent-child relationship that exists between her new husband and his children. His relationship with them may be stronger than his relationship with her.

Third is the awareness stage, in which stepparents begin to sort out their feelings and put names to their experiences. They admit they can't always like their stepchildren, or that they can't do it all. Often this is the first time they are able to verbalize their feelings.

The fourth stage is mobilization, in which stepparents speak up for themselves and make their demands known. It is usually a period of considerable conflict. In the fifth stage, action, the family group begins to move away from being a primarily biologically-organized group toward being a functioning stepfamily. Stepparents at this time begin to form more satisfying relationships with their stepchildren, relationships not dependent on the spouse for approval.

Stage six is contact, in which the stepparents engage in more intense and satisfying one-to-one contacts with both their stepchildren and their spouses. For instance, the stepmother and the father develop a stronger bond, which diffuses the father's bond with his children but at the same time "allows" the stepmother to begin to establish relationships with her stepchildren. As the bond between the parents becomes stronger the stepmother can establish more intimate and satisfying relationships with her stepchildren.

The final stage is resolution, in which the stepparent is able to both "hold on" to and yet "let go" of the stepchild, while experiencing a solid primary adult-couple relationship. Altogether, these stages take from four to seven years, in Papernow's study, about four years in "fast" families, seven in "average" families. Some families take longer.

Designating the stages that a stepfamily goes through is helpful in that one can see that there is a process of adjustment that is normal even if it is stressful. Papernow's "Stepfamily Cycle" underlines the differences between a stepfamily and a biological family. It shows how periods of anxiety and anger are to be expected and can be utilized to bring the stepfamily along to another stage of family development.

An important aspect of Papernow's study is that the stepfamily takes time to "adjust to itself." Most therapists agree that it takes at least two years for the stepfamily even to begin to adjust to its new relationships, and many stepfamilies take years before they have come to a satisfying family unit.

Edmund Burke called time the "grand Instructor," and Disraeli said that it is the "great physician." Time, for a stepfamily, does instruct and heal. When a stepfamily is formed there is much to be learned while the family members are recovering from loss and forming a new family unit.

The stepfamily, just like the characters in the old fairy tales, has obstacles to overcome—the dragon of jealousy to slay, the wicked stepmother of resentment to destroy, the giants of fear and guilt to do away with. And just as fairy-tale characters find themselves in hostile and dark forests, the stepfamily is often in the dark, with no guideposts in the form of the rules, rituals, and support systems that are such a vital part of the biological step's sense of identity.

Most stepmothers feel isolated and alone with their problems. They don't know where to go for help, and feel that no one could possibly understand what they are experiencing. According to Papernow, the stepparent trying to guide and help the family toward unity needs outside support. She states:

> Support here is defined as the presence of another person, or persons, with whom the step-

parent could talk openly about his or her stepping experience, who could hear the stepparent's
feelings and perceptions without judging or pressur-
ing him or her to be different, and who could help
stepparents to differentiate their style, experience,
and needs from that of the biological units they
joined.[6]

Papernow goes on to say that in her study support from
the spouse provided the best insurance of movement through
the cycle, and stepparents who were strongly supported by
their spouse experienced less anguish and shame. Without
spousal support, stepparents either turned to the outside for
help (as Nancy returned to AA) or experienced such acute
problems that their marriage was endangered.

Although the best help for a stepmother may be from the
person who brought her into a stepfamily in the first place—
her husband—if he is unable to give support then she must find
it somewhere else. A family therapist is one solution if the
therapist is experienced with stepfamilies. If not, they may
place unrealistic expectations on stepparents. Many stepmothers feel that going to a therapist admits failure on their part.
The realization that she has taken on a herculean task, which is
made even more difficult by the lack of societal guidelines, can
enable the stepmother to seek professional help. Family therapists admit, however, that they too are just beginning to
understand the complexities of a stepfamily and how it differs
from a biological family. The Stepfamily Association of America in Baltimore, Maryland, is an invaluable resource. Local
chapters provide education/support meetings, usually once a
month. The S.A.A. publishes the *Stepfamily Bulletin,* which
comes out quarterly and contains articles, stories, and support
for people in these roles.

The stepmother can also work to establish her own support
group by organizing other stepmothers. Most stepmothers are
convinced that perhaps no one but another stepmother can
understand what they are experiencing, and to some extent
they are right. Talking about the problems, expressing negative feelings, is of great importance during times of stress.

Even a single friend outside the family can help if he or she is nonjudgmental and understanding.

It can be very destructive, however, if a stepmother turns to a family member other than her husband to air her problems. It is too great a burden on a child to hear of a mother's anxiety and resentment, and the members of a stepmother's own family of origin will be much too likely to take sides and polarize the individuals.

As a stepmother considers her husband, her children, and herself in establishing a home, she can set certain "tasks" involving these individuals as she works toward family unity.

Repeatedly, an open and nurturing relationship with her husband is seen to be essential for a stepmother. The term "primary love relationship" is apt, for if this bond is severed the stepfamily has no possibility of surviving as a unit. Therapists generally agree that in order for this relationship to be healthy certain boundaries must be established between parents and children, both physical and emotional. This is easier said than done, since initially parents have stronger bonds with their biological children than with their new spouses. Even closing the bedroom door can seem like a hostile act to a child who is used to moving in and out of a single parent's bedroom or even sleeping with them from time to time.

The instinctive protectiveness of a biological parent is another barrier between the remarried couple. Many stepmothers find their new husbands to be defensive about their biological children's behavior and nonsupportive of the stepmother's disciplinary actions. Although this is normal, at least initially, the couple needs to work to form a united front so that children are not allowed to play one partner off against the other. Being open with her husband—expressing her needs, her own sense of confusion, and sometimes her shame at her negative feelings—is one of the primary tasks of a stepmother.

Secondly, a stepmother needs to work toward establishing her particular role with her stepchildren. Although she is not the biological mother, she can develop a special relationship with her stepchildren that can be satisfying in its own way. Stepmothers sometimes refer to themselves as fulfilling the role of friend, teacher, or mentor; one stepmother said she felt like an aunt, a comparison that in many ways comes closer to the stepmother's role than the other terms. Like an aunt, the stepmother is related to the children, although more distantly than immediate family. An aunt has a close relationship to a parent, just like a stepmother. An aunt is an acknowledged part of the family but has some distance from the bond of a parent and child. With an aunt a child can form a close relationship that has a separate quality from that with a parent. A "favorite aunt" implies the existence of an extended family, which in some ways a stepfamily is.

Whatever role the stepmother finds with her stepchildren, it must be an expression of her individual style and method of expression. Most therapists agree that her role must be "adult," and must be actively supported by her spouse.

It seems fair to say that as stepmothers try to maintain their own self-esteem while working through the steps of establishing healthy family relationships, they cannot "go it alone." They need the support of their husbands first of all, but may also need outside support in the form of groups, close friends, or counseling. Stepmothers owe it to themselves and to their families to speak out, seek help, and establish a comfortable place for themselves. Stepmothers will find that within them lurks both the wicked stepmother and the saintly Snow White, but with time and support they will be able to go beyond either image. This does not mean that everyone will live happily ever after, as reported in the fairy tales, but rather, in family systems terms, that the stepfamily can take steps toward healthy family unity.

The stepmother needs to realize that she is still in relatively uncharted territory. She is most often thrown back on her own resources, although help is on the way. Meanwhile, everything from reexamining centuries-old fairy tales to studying the most recent literature on family therapy can help her understand that stress is normal. By understanding the underlying reasons for this stress, she can help herself progress along the stages of stepparenthood.

After all is said and done, the term "step" may still be the most appropriate. There are definite steps that stepmothers, stepfathers, and stepchildren must take in order to become healthy stepfamilies. It is a process, a movement forward, one step at a time. The family can be in step and out of step at any given moment but as long as it continues moving it is a viable living unit. The stepfamily that works toward cohesion can feel proud, because it is through choice and active participation that the family will find success. By recognizing that the family needs to move forward one step at a time, and that the development will take time, the stepmother can better understand the process of "stepping."

6

Money

*TAKING THE EVIL OUT OF
THE NECESSARY*

"MONEY MAKES THE WORLD GO AROUND." THIS APPOSITE SONG FROM THE musical and movie *Cabaret* could well be sung at high pitch in most stepfamily situations. Money doesn't just make the step-family's world go around, it makes it go back and forth, up and down, and spin in upon itself with dizzying reverberations. It is almost impossible to satisfy everyone in money matters and often no one is satisfied. The ex-wife needs more. Teenage children complain that their stepmother is first in line for the bucks. Adult children fear that the new wife will end up with what they consider their rightful inheritance. Meanwhile, the stepmother often sees her hard-earned money going out for alimony and child-support payments.

In money matters the human qualities of self-interest and survival can take on their most negative forms. Money isn't all bad, however. It can also be a means of positive communication and commitment, a way of showing love and giving protection. Just as a dollar bill represents what is behind it, money represents much more than purchasing power.

74

At the most basic level, money is necessary for survival. Long gone are the days when America was primarily agrarian and people could achieve a degree of self-sufficiency from the land. Ours is a consumer society; you get what you pay for and not much more. Housing, food, clothing, all the physical essentials of life have to be purchased. Medical, legal, educational, and insurance services must be bought.

Most families depend on two wage-earners in order to meet these financial obligations. In both biological families and stepfamilies mothers often need to contribute financially just to keep up with expenses. Many stepmothers find that in addition to trying to befriend or nurture their new family, it is also necessary to help pay the bills.

In society we are often defined by what we are able to purchase. Therefore we are dependent on money; with money we have a degree of security and power and without it we feel powerless. A man who won the New York State lottery said that one of the best things about having money was being able to get in a taxi in Manhattan and tell the driver to take him to his apartment far out in Brooklyn. It wasn't that he couldn't afford the taxi ride before he won the lottery, but having so *much* money behind him gave him the sense of power necessary to insist that the taxi-driver take him home.

This story is interesting because it implies what money does. The lottery-winner had the same right and enough money to take a taxi to Brooklyn before he won a million dollars, but he somehow did not feel he had the power to insist on the ride home. Money can make you feel comfortable and assured, whereas lack of it can make you defensive, afraid, and sometimes even a little paranoid.

The lack of money, or the *perceived* lack of it, often causes a great deal of conflict in the stepfamily. Although parental roles are changing in our society, and most families depend on two paychecks for survival, it is still usually the father who is the primary wage-earner in a family, and a stepmother marries a father. This father has children with needs, and these children have a mother to whom the father is still legally bound financially. In a real sense, although no longer joined with his ex-wife in a mutual life commitment, he holds power over her and her children. Understanding their position of dependency is crucial for a stepmother, because dependency rarely inspires gratitude but rather can breed fear, anger, and a desperate need to "look out for number one."

I remember how desperate I felt when I was living alone in New York City with my two young children. I had asked for no alimony and the child-support payments were just enough to keep me solvent. When no child-support payments came for three months and the rent was due, I felt panic. When I called my estranged husband, he angrily responded, "I'm strapped right now for cash. Why don't you get some money from your parents?"

Although I could have asked my parents for a loan, I felt it would be starting a precedent that would eventually make me dependent on them. I had a job and I was determined to make it on my own. However, the child-support payments were an essential part of my budget. Without them I felt trapped, and felt put in the position of having to *ask* for money. I felt powerless to do anything but call again and try to insist on a payment.

I was, in a sense, dependent on the kindness of others. It is a helpless feeling. When repeated requests got no results, I filed suit in family court. It was a very low point in my life. As I faced the terrifying specter of having to borrow and make excuses and beg for each monthly check, I was reminded of a line from Shaw's play *Major Barbara:* "Money is the most important thing in the world. It represents health, strength, honor, generosity, and beauty as conspicuously as the want of it represents illness, weakness, disgrace, meanness, and ugliness."

Whether or not money in fact represents all the positive qualities Shaw attributed to it, certainly "weakness, disgrace, meanness, and ugliness" took on a particular meaning as I faced my ex-husband in the squalid surroundings of family court. What had happened to us that we should find ourselves there? We were responsible, capable adults who had managed to work through most of our separation amicably. But as too often happens in divorce, there are times when things do not go smoothly, and often the problems involve money.

In a few years the shoe was on the other foot. After Lee and I were married we had a series of court battles with his ex-wife over finances. Although we won the cases, the costs were high. We could have financed a year's college tuition on the total legal costs alone. And emotional costs were high as well. Lee would use all his patience trying to talk things out with his ex-wife's lawyer and then hang up the phone and get angry at me. I found myself angry at Lee for signing such a horrible separation agreement in the first place. It seemed as though he had promised to give up everything because he was leaving his marriage and I had asked for nothing because I was leaving mine. Hasty financial arrangements invariably do not work out, and the renegotiations often involve much bitterness and expensive legal battles.

Unfortunately, our situation is more the norm than the exception. Court expenses are often a harsh reality in stepfamily life. Chances are very good that a stepmother will become involved in court proceedings, whether because of her own divorce or her husband's. Going to court costs money, time, and emotion. You have to hire a lawyer, take time off from work to attend hearings and perhaps trials, and you may have to explain all your finances to a hostile lawyer or spend inordinate amounts of money settling disputes over such basic things as visitation rights.

The use of the legal system to solve financial problems within the family is distasteful for everyone, but it is sometimes the only way to find a solution. Because the use and abuse of money carry with them such heavy emotional baggage, some problems can only be solved through an impersonal, dispassionate party.

Ideally, an equitable financial arrangement can be made at the time of divorce, but since circumstances change over time, some agreements may have to be renegotiated. Although a stepmother can encourage her husband to reexamine his divorce agreement, or can attempt to help him work out a more realistic financial arrangement with his ex-wife, usually the best thing she can do is stay out of it as much as possible. It is, after all, his problem, and one he must work through as best he can. In the end, there is probably very little she can do anyway, and her involvement will often seem to be an attempt to get more money for herself.

Although it may be advisable to distance oneself from financial arrangements with one's husband's ex-wife, a step-mother cannot help but be directly involved in money decisions concerning stepchildren. Her understanding of the financial relationship between her husband and his children is of the utmost importance, and here the stepmother needs to be sensitive to her husband's deeply felt emotions as a father.

A young stepmother, Natalie, made some observations about her husband's relationship with his children that helped her deal with financial arrangements more realistically. Her story is particularly interesting because it goes beyond the dreary minutiae of dollars and cents and examines how money can be a positive expression of caring.

Natalie considered herself a radical feminist who wanted primarily to be financially independent. An accomplished artist, she loved teaching children but had no desire to give birth. When she met John, he was still married and had two children aged three and five. As their relationship progressed and they fell in love, she felt that his son and daughter, Tommy and Fran, would be the perfect compromise: she could express her mothering instincts but would not have children who would interfere with her professional career.

As is often the case in a divorce in which one spouse perceives him- or herself as leaving the marriage, John felt a tremendous sense of guilt when he left his wife of ten years. When his three-year-old son begged, "I promise I'll be a good boy if you come back," he was truly in pain. He wanted his ex-wife and children to have everything since they couldn't have him, and so he promised to give them practically his entire salary.

Although he felt strongly that the children's place was with their mother, he missed them terribly. They visited him every other weekend but, as he admitted to Natalie, he missed them every single day. He was also concerned about their welfare. His ex-wife was struggling to overcome alcoholism while she worked and went to school part-time. John often felt that he was the only one in the world who could really protect them.

Natalie was convinced that John was unreasonable about what he owed his children. She and he rented an apartment with two bedrooms and the children got the bigger one. It did not matter to John that the room was empty twelve days out of fourteen, it was important that Tommy and Fran had the big room and that they felt it was theirs. When they visited, John was anxious to be the chief nurturer and care-giver. He would be up before everyone preparing a big breakfast, and would plan outings and shopping trips for the children. He never asked Natalie to do anything alone with them and would even go out of his way not to leave her with them. Natalie felt that John stood in the way of her forming a close relationship with his children. He served as a conduit through which she experienced them, but she was kept at bay. She began to dread the weekend visits; not only did she feel displaced, but also her husband was filled with anxiety. On Wednesday John would seem distracted, by Thursday he would start to withdraw, and by Friday a blue funk would settle over the apartment. It seemed to Natalie that nothing could comfort John regarding his children. He was miserable without them and unhappy when they came to visit.

Natalie says the first two years of her marriage were terrible in many ways. She was experiencing, with John, all the pain, remorse, and fear of a man leaving his family. She could not understand it or, on a basic level, relate to it.

They decided to go into therapy and chose a controversial but, for them, effective system called "forced holding." As the term implies, part of the therapy involves holding someone down physically until they become angry enough to release deeply felt emotions. Once when John was holding her, Natalie yelled at him, "You don't want me to even be alone with your children! You're afraid I'll kill them!"

John agreed that he wanted to protect them from her. He

did feel that she might be cruel to them, since they were really not her children. He insisted that she could not know what it was really like to have her own child. As they talked, he began to express his fears for Tommy and Fran. He worried about them: worried when they were with their mother, worried when they were taking the bus down for their visit, worried even when they were with Natalie. His greatest need was to protect them and being separated from them gave him constant anxiety. His love for them was based on the primary kinship bond of parent and child, and his sense of guilt and sadness at being separated from them manifested itself in his fear and suspicion of her.

After two years of marriage Natalie decided that she did want to have a child. John agreed, and they began to plan their future. They borrowed enough money to build a house big enough for the new child and for two small bedrooms for his children. A house of this size meant Natalie would have to keep working full-time even after the baby was born. She agreed without reservation.

They built the new house, and Natalie had a son. She returned to full-time work just as they had planned. She put her son in day care and then found that she missed him so much she would break into tears at the slightest cause. She hated being separated from him and spent hours at work worrying that he wasn't being treated well enough. She wished she could afford a better day-care center or a full-time baby-sitter. She wished she had enough money to stay at home and take care of him herself.

Having her own child made her realize what John had been going through with his own two children. Being separated from them, he had so few ways to connect, to show them love and to protect them ... and one of these ways was money.

She also admitted that although she and John had worked through many of their problems, she still found herself looking at a price tag for something he had bought Tommy or Fran and figuring out how many hours she had had to spend working and away from her son in order for him to buy it. Recognizing this in herself, she could appreciate why John felt so uncertain about her with his children. Of course John was right to fear her, in a way. She could see, after having her own child, that her need to protect her son far surpassed any protectiveness she felt for her stepchildren. She liked them, wanted to do things with them, but she did not feel an almost blind need to protect them.

John and Natalie's experience points out some of the most fundamental aspects of stepfamily relationships vis-à-vis money: first, the pain and often guilt a father feels when he leaves his children. He cannot be with them, he misses them, and he also wants to make it up somehow, both to make himself feel better and to make things easier for his children. One of the few ways he can do this is to make sure there is enough money to make up for the fact that he is not there.

Instinctively, he hopes money will protect them, and protection is a primary feeling in most parents. We all try to buy protection for our children—it can take the form of everything from dental care or hiring tutors to a pretty blouse or a BMX bicycle. We want them to look acceptable so other children won't make fun of them. We want them to have the same toys or bicycles so they won't feel neglected. We can all dream up a million expensive ways to protect our children . . . but the basic desire to protect is much stronger in a natural parent than in a stepparent.

This desire to protect is *not* the same thing as "buying love." Although guilt may play a part, the basic instinct is to give, not buy. A parent who wants to give and protect should not be made to feel guilty for his parental desire.

It is helpful for a stepmother to realize that her feelings toward her stepchildren, even though they may be fair and positive, are different from those of her husband. An interesting aspect of the wicked stepmother of fairy tales is that she often has the ability to turn the father against his own children. Too often, stepchildren perceive their stepmother as insisting that she come first financially. Although this perception may be unfair, a stepmother may need to bend over

backward in order to help her husband show love and commitment to his children. To receive understanding from his wife
will help ease the pain he feels in being separated from them.

When stepchildren live in the family the situation is
different. Most stepparents agree that it is always financially
easier with people living under the same roof. They are sharing
the same food, the same rooms, and even if the needs for braces
or clothes or tutors are different, they do not seem so very
different from a biological family's needs.

Problems do arise, however. Often in stepfamilies some
members have access to more money than others, and inequities
inevitably arise. After our divorce my ex-husband eventually
moved to California, where he became a very successful
scriptwriter. To my daughter Kris he was able to offer luxuries
that were impossible for Lee's children or for our two children,
Adam and Miranda. Kris was given trips to Europe and
Russia, vacations in California, and an education at one of the
most expensive colleges in America. We simply could not do
this for the other children. They were expected to help pay
their own way through college, to contribute to household
expenses when they lived with us as young adults, and when it
came time for our son Adam to look at colleges, it was difficult
to offer him the same opportunity that Kris had been given. At
the same time, it would have been unfair to expect Kris not to
take advantage of her father's largess.

The opposite was true for Lee's children. Their mother
worked part-time and a lot of her income was alimony and
child-support payments from Lee. Lee is an artist, with a
fluctuating income. Our children's needs did not necessarily
coincide with our ability to cover expenses. We were less able
to help Lee's older sons financially than we were his younger
daughter, simply because our financial situation improved as
time went on. The well-known quote "All are equal, but some
are more equal than others" is often the case in stepfamilies.
Still, one cannot tally up each child's expenses and try to see
that everyone gets the same. As a stepmother with a family of
six says, "At Christmas, our ten-year-old wanted a bike and he
was ready for one. A good bike can cost $200. To be fair we

would have to spend that on each child, but six times $200? There was no way we could do that!"

These inevitable inequities, coupled with the sense of insecurity that often affects children of divorce, can make both children and teenagers seem excessively selfish and manipulative. One stepmother remembers how her stepson acted at the dinner table: "Sam was frantic to be sure he got the first helping and constantly asked if there was more in the kitchen. If I made cookies, he grabbed handfuls of them before they were even cool. I think he felt deprived, somehow, because of his parents' divorce . . . and he had a fear of being 'cut out.' That sense of deprivation which manifested itself in physical things must have been based in something much more emotional. There was absolutely no cause for him to worry about there being enough food . . . but he acted like every meal was his last."

The child playing in a sandbox, holding on to his toy truck and screaming "mine!," is a common sight. Childhood is a time of self-interest, and it is only through the maturing process that we learn to be generous and sharing. Children who have experienced divorce cannot help but feel the tensions involved in the division of material goods and the almost inevitable need of the parents to get what they can financially from the settlement. At the same time, the children feel emotionally deprived because they have lost what was familiar and important to them, their original family. The result sometimes makes children continue or return to the childish behavior of selfishness. They feel they have to look out for number one.

As children move into their teenage years this behavior can become much more sophisticated. They can become particularly adept at maneuvering and manipulating their parents for money. They grow much more aware of the emotional content of money, and their financial needs are usually greater than those of younger children. They are trying to become independent at a time when they are still financially dependent, which is frustrating for everyone.

In any family the child's move toward independence is tied to dependency on money. Even a relatively young child finds pleasure in having his or her own money, and if children can be given a positive sense of control over their finances, it can help to ease the emotional frustration they feel. It doesn't have to be a large amount, but money can be something they can control—which can be important for children of divorce. Although it's nice to talk about all being a family and sharing, it is probably more practical to pay children for their contribution to family life rather than expect that they will help simply for the good of the household.

Most families try to divide up chores that need to be done, such as setting the table, washing dishes, taking out the garbage. These chores are usually rewarded with an allowance, which is fixed according to the child's age and ability to help. Outside of these general chores, there are others that can be done for extra money. Children over ten can do their own laundry, be in charge of baking cookies, be responsible for cleaning the family room, or do regular yard work. These larger jobs should get more pay and an effort should be found to help the children earn more money as their needs increase. Baby-sitting, odd jobs for neighbors, or anything that will give a child some outside income should be encouraged. The more money children have that they feel is totally their own, the less powerless and frustrated they will feel.

It is also possible that encouraging teenagers to earn extra money can help strengthen their bond with the stepfamily. If they can take care of their personal needs themselves, there is less drain on family finances in general, and in this way the teenager is actually participating in meeting family financial obligations. Not only is it pleasant to feel that one can take care of oneself to some extent, it is also a positive feeling to know that one is helping the family. Giving a teenager this sense of family participation can help the adolescent feel that he or she is a constructive part of the new family.

It is easy enough to advise families about financial matters, but daily life presents an unending list of needs, negotiations, and compromises. A stepmother is only human and she cannot be immune to her own financial concerns.

No matter how philosophically a stepmother views alimony and child support, every penny that goes out for her husband's ex-wife and family is money taken away from her own personal needs and the needs of her own children. And in the end, often no one is satisfied: the ex-wife rarely feels that payments are enough to meet her needs, the stepmother feels the strain of seeing large amounts of money leave the family coffers, and the father feels pulled back and forth with the responsibilities of his two families. The children almost invariably feel that they are getting short shrift in the money exchange. It is hard to create a feeling of "we are all in this together and must help each other out." More often one sees a group of individuals who, like Sam, try to get the first helping in case there's no more in the kitchen. None of us are attractive when we are haggling about money.

A stepmother usually has little to say about her husband's divorce settlement and simply has to live with it. She also has little to say about his deeply felt emotional need to protect his children. And she cannot prepare herself for her protective needs toward her own children.

So what's a stepmother to do? There are no pat answers to the quagmire of stepfamily financial problems. It may be helpful, however, to divide financial affairs into two separate categories, those over which the stepmother has some control and those over which she doesn't. There is a popular prayer that asks for help in changing what can be changed and in leaving what cannot be changed, and for the wisdom to know the difference. The key is having the wisdom to know the difference.

For the stepmother, this usually means standing back from her husband's financial relationship with his ex-wife and children and concentrating on her own financial needs. Although this may initially sound selfish, giving her husband the sense of support he needs to work out his finances is most generous.

At the same time, a stepmother needs to decide realistically what she believes is fair for herself and her children and to work to find a means toward that arrangement. The parents need to work to be fair and to communicate to their children their overall aim. To whatever extent possible, children should be included in family financial discussions so that they have some understanding of the reality of the family's finances. They need to be made aware of their parents' financial goals even if they may not agree with them. They should know that money is being saved for college or is being used to pay for the new house or has been set aside for taxes and insurance. Without this overall sense of what the money is being used for, everyone will be grabbing for a piece of the pie, with little regard for other family members.

As with all families, stepfamilies must work out a budget of sorts and designate who actually pays the bills. This varies from family to family. In our family, I keep the family accounts and pay the bills. In some families the father has this responsibility. Another possibility that often works well in stepfamilies is a kind of "financial separation" of the married couple.

This method can help take the emotional content out of the checkbook. The arrangements are quite simple. A couple agrees that one of them will pay certain bills, usually the bills that that spouse has either more interest in or more control over, and the other spouse agrees to pay the other bills. Both work out their own budget with enough extra allowed for at least some discretionary monies. The couple keeps two separate accounts and two separate checkbooks. These accounts are not based on the separate income of the partners but rather on the expenses that they have agreed to be responsible for. Each partner knows how much he or she has and can make decisions on how the money should be spent.

The beauty of this arrangement is that no one has to make excuses, explain bills, or feel that someone is disapprovingly looking over one's shoulder. One does not need to know the Visa bill or the stepchildren's dentist bill or whatever, unless one wants to make a special effort. If an agreement can be reached on how to divide the monthly income and who will be responsible for what payments, financial tensions can be alleviated.

Sometimes it's just better not to have to see an amount

deducted directly from your balance, even if you know in the back of your head how much is going out of the family funds. Seeing a stepchild appear in a brand-new pair of designer jeans can be easier if the price of those jeans remains a little vague. Ignorance may not be bliss, but not focusing on certain details can sometimes be easier.

What you do know is that you and your husband are working to build a family, a family that won't fit into the traditional patterns. It is a disrupted family, a rejoined family, a disjointed family, and a combined family. Within this family are all the emotions of love, guilt, hope, ambition, anger, and deprivation, and sometimes these emotions can only find expression through the uses and abuses of money. Given the fact that most stepfamilies, by the very nature of their existence, have less money to go around, it is most important to find both creative financing and ways to circumvent the emotional mine-field of monetary matters. As Lord Rutherford said, "We haven't the money, so we've got to think."

Money is good and money is bad. Understanding that it is good when used as a sign of love and commitment or to give a sense of security, and bad when used to express resentment, anger, or power, a stepmother can work to find a clear-cut method of viewing money. It is necessary but it does not have to be a necessary evil.

7

The Ex-Wife

AND ALL THAT THAT IMPLIES

"I HAVE REALLY MADE AN EFFORT TO BE FAIR AND REASONABLE WITH MY ex-husband. I honestly think I am the ideal ex-wife. But my husband's ex-wife . . . what a bitch!"

Most of us who are both ex-wives and present wives feel this way at least some of the time. No matter how hard we try to be objective and fair about the "other woman" in our husband's life, her presence is not only a fact of our existence together but often also an intrusive presence. She is present in her children, in her financial needs, and in her emotional claim on the people in a stepfamily.

Just as all stepmothers cannot be as wicked as the myths claim, all ex-wives cannot be as horrible as second wives claim. It is clear, however, that there is often a pattern of at least some degree of hostility between second wives and ex-wives. A stepmother not only marries a father, she also marries someone else's husband. The "ex-" before the term does not obviate the fact that the husband previously made marriage vows and lived in the married state with a different woman. He and this woman have conceived and brought into the world children, and they are therefore intrinsically bound together in a way that all the legalities in the world cannot totally negate. This does not necessarily mean that he still loves or even likes her, but he is nevertheless still in some ways bound to her.

Although an ex-wife is not officially a member of the stepfamily household, she is often a "silent partner," and her influence and, often, her power can be pervasive. Although her relationship to her ex-husband has been legally reduced to alimony, child support, or both, the arrangements can still produce complexity and strain. After all, the relationship is still bound by money on one hand and love (for the child) on the other.

It is tempting to divide ex-wives into categories such as "overdependent," "hostile," or "mentally disturbed," in other words categories that designate them as bad, worse, and worst of all. Just like stepmothers, ex-wives often get a bad rap, and a consistently negative attitude toward another individual is destructive in the long run.

The stepmother's relationship with the ex-wife involves two major aspects of her life—her husband and her stepchildren. If an ex-wife is unmarried, her needs are usually somewhat different from those of a remarried woman: they tend to be more emotional. Most stepmothers interviewed found the unmarried ex-wife difficult, and since Lee's ex-wife never remarried, I am most familiar with this situation. Lee and I fell in love while we were both married to other people so our relationship with his ex-wife was particularly strained. For her I was the archetypal "other woman" who had destroyed a marriage. Although healthy marriages are not destroyed by outsiders, I nevertheless found myself constantly on the defensive. I am sure that if one compared Lee's ex-wife's version of what happened with my version, it would not sound like the same situation at all. Without trying to analyze who has been right or wrong over the years, certain "truths" have become evident for me.

It seems to me that there was continuous anger in our relationship with Lee's former wife. Long-term, festering anger clouds one's ability to see clearly. It becomes, like jealousy, a monster that feeds on itself. It has the ability to become like a narcotic, demanding more and more attention and energy that should be directed toward more positive things. Any ex-wife who is making life difficult, for whatever reason, can become someone we all "love to hate," and even though joining together against what seem to be her unreasonable demands can lend a relationship a sense of excitement and unity, it gives nobody ultimate satisfaction. It can put the married couple on the defensive, so that the message to the children becomes "Whoever is not with us is against us," which is unfair to them. In a relationship in which there is anger, hostility, and revenge, no one comes out ahead.

In my own case, in addition to the anger I felt, I remember feeling intensely competitive. I wanted to outshine Lee's former wife on all fronts, as if by doing so I could prove to myself and to the world that he was right in leaving her for me. Anything that was bad in his former marriage I did not want in ours. Anything that was good, I wanted to be better.

Lee's daughter Kate had been born at home, and he had found it a wonderful experience. We decided our second child should also be born at home and I was determined to make that an even *more* rewarding experience. I have no doubt that the psychological determination to have a wonderful, easy birth made our daughter Miranda's birth at home the happiest and easiest I ever experienced. The strength of that determination was greater than any painkiller developed by science.

In my experience with stepmothers, I have found that this same kind of determination will make a woman take on herculean tasks in order to prove herself better than an ex-wife. Not only does she want to be a better mother, she often wants to do better professionally and to be more attractive physically. Unfortunately, the determination to surpass the ex-wife can result in unnecessary disappointment and a sense of failure. And after all is said and done, outdoing your husband's ex-wife is an empty victory, because instead of concentrating on the positive aspects of your marital relationship you are concentrating on achieving a goal that makes another individual look deficient. At the same time, this allows the other person to have undue influence in your life.

Looking back, I can now see years of negative energy spent on the emotional battlefield. Perhaps much of what happened was inevitable, but at some point I finally achieved an emotional distance and an ability to be somewhat detached. This has made all the difference.

What I can now see, at least for a divorced woman who does not remarry, is the ex-wife's sense of loss, not only of her husband but also of her home and her singular claim as the mother of his children. This loss can never be recovered, and only when a woman "lets it all go" and begins to build a new life for herself can she feel whole again. A stepmother is not in a position to effect this change in an ex-wife, however. It is out of her control.

There is another, subtler emotion that often exists between divorced couples. It is the particular romantic memory that we often have for someone we have once loved. It is a wonderful fantasy to think that someone you once loved and who loved you, even if that love ended in bitterness, might see you again one day in the future and say, "Ah, we had some good times. You will always have a special place in my heart." It's that scene in the film *The Way We Were* when Robert Redford sees Barbra Streisand on the street, years after their divorce. The notion that this might happen gives some justification to that early commitment and also has a bittersweet, sentimental quality to it. The fantasy is based not so much on one's own feelings toward the past lover as on a need for a sense of self-worth, a kind of romantic validation.

I believe many ex-wives have some variation on this fantasy. I know I did. Even though I knew I wanted a divorce and had no question about my love for Lee, I couldn't help but want to think that I would somehow always be special in my first husband's eyes. I was fascinated by the women he married after me and could not help but compare them to myself in my mind.

Unrealistic, yes. Childish, perhaps so. But at least I grew to recognize these kinds of emotions, and that helped me understand the many dimensions of the dynamic that existed between Lee and his former wife.

Know thyself. To thine own self be true. These aphorisms are particularly apt when you are dealing with ex-wives. It is important to separate your problems from her problems. Most stepmothers feel that they have no control over decisions made by their husbands' ex-wives, although those decisions affect their own lives. To a great extent this is true. If an ex-wife decides to deny visitation rights in order to obtain more child support (a fairly common occurrence), or if she makes what seem to be unreasonable financial demands, or constantly calls for help with everything from the plumbing to Johnny's grade in school, there is not much a stepmother can do. As was discussed in the chapter on money, there are certain areas that remain primarily between your husband and his ex-wife. You can be supportive and helpful to him in whatever way you see fit, but jumping into the fray by demanding that she not call again, or taking it upon yourself to tell her to leave you alone, will only draw you into a three-way battle. Step back and let him deal with her, if at all possible.

Not all husbands have troubles with their ex-wives, of course. People who were not able to stay married sometimes find that they can nevertheless be good friends. Although it takes a degree of self-confidence to feel comfortable while your husband is spending pleasant time with his ex-wife, it is important to remember how much more constructive for everyone this kind of relationship is. One stepmother tells of how she, her husband, and his ex-wife were together at a party. Her husband introduced them to a friend of his by saying, "Here are the two most wonderful women a man could be married to."

There should be room in a man's life for two of the "most wonderful women," and as long as the stepmother concentrates on her own relationship with her husband, rather than trying to negate his relationship with his ex, she is moving forward in the stages of developing a healthy stepfamily life.

One stepmother who was interviewed not only felt comfortable with her husband's close relationship with his ex-wife, but she found that she also grew to look to her for advice and help with the children. Although the mother moved out of the house after the divorce, she remained close enough for the children to visit her. Sally, the stepmother, was considerably younger than her husband, and did not feel confident as a mother, even though the two children lived with her. Not only was her husband David's divorce amicable but his ex-wife, Eleanor, was unusually supportive of the new marriage. Eleanor told her children, "If you don't like Sally you won't be betraying your father, and if you do like her you won't be betraying me."

Sally moved into the house that had been bought and furnished by David and Eleanor and accepted the family routines that had been established. She is an actress, and she found that she could develop a comfortable relationship with her stepchildren (ages eleven and fifteen) by being involved with them in the community theater. This was their own special activity together that was different from what they did with their mother.

Sally was able to accept Eleanor's continued presence in the family because she did not see herself as a mother but rather as an older sister or friend. She looked to Eleanor as the family mother-figure, helping her as well as the two children. Sally was in love with David and her relationship with him was the most important thing to her. She felt satisfied to share her love of theater with her stepchildren but did not feel the need to mother them.

In my experience, Sally is by far more the exception than the norm. Although the divorce rate is so high that more and more women are marrying fathers, women need to examine their reasons for marrying a man with children. One assumes that the marriage takes place because the two people are in love, but a closer self-examination may indicate that other factors are involved. Many women state that they married a "family," or that they hoped their husband's children would fulfill their need for motherhood.

Diana, a nurse, admits that her husband Alex's seven-year-old daughter was one of the reasons she was so attracted to him. Although Alex made it very clear during their courtship that he would have no more children, Diana didn't mind, because there was already his daughter, Laura. Laura lived with her mother, Molly, who had remarried and given birth to three more children. Because Molly's present husband had a disability and worked sporadically, their family income was meager. They lived in a trailer on the outskirts of a town known for its high unemployment and crime rate.

When Diana first met Laura, her heart went out to her. Here was this charming child who came to visit her father in soiled clothes smelling of baby vomit and spoiled milk. As she talked with Laura, Diana realized that this seven-year-old spent most of her free time taking care of babies or helping with household chores. Diana could imagine the trailer filled with little children who needed constant attention, a stepfather who was sick at home much of the time, and a mother distracted and overworked. She sensed Laura's need for individual nurturing and attention, and felt she could take care of her stepdaughter and give her a new life.

Laura was thrilled about being a part of Diana and Alex's wedding. Diana helped her buy a new dress and shoes and spent time with her before the ceremony, helping her dress and fixing her hair.

After the wedding Diana occasionally let Laura visit her at work in the hospital, introducing her to the nurses and doctors and letting her run small errands. When Alex and Diana built a new house they included an extra bedroom for Laura's weekend visits. Diana altered her nurse uniforms for Laura and gave her stepdaughter charts and bottles that she could use to play nurse. They shopped for clothes, toiletries, and educational games. Diana showed Laura how to practice basic personal hygiene, everything from cutting her toenails to washing her hair. When Diana insisted that Laura bathe every night and would not allow her to wear soiled clothes, Laura seemed to react positively, as though she was pleased that someone really cared about how she looked.

Soon after Diana's marriage, Laura's mother had another baby, and it became evident that Laura was having trouble in school. Diana set up a schedule of study time with her but soon realized that Laura's problems reflected her home environment rather than her intelligence. A few hours on a weekend were not enough to compensate for the time Laura spent helping her mother with the babies. Diana hoped that Laura would choose to live with her and Alex so she could really help her. She carefully suggested to Laura that she was welcome to live there if she wished.

Laura, however, never complained about her life with her mother or indicated that she wanted to live with Diana and Alex. Her mother, Molly, on the other hand, seemed to resent Diana's influence on Laura. Molly gathered up all the clothes Diana had bought for Laura and gave them to the Salvation Army, insisting that Laura had outgrown them. Sometimes she would not let Alex take Laura for the weekend, saying that the child had work to do at home and couldn't leave. The situation became increasingly difficult, with Molly often denying Alex the right to see his daughter, or Laura arriving dirty and exhausted for a visit and afraid to take any of Diana's gifts. On Sunday afternoons a great gloom would settle over the family as Laura carefully chose a few things to take back with her, or as she explained that perhaps she would not be able to visit the next weekend unless the baby got well, etc. But she never asked to stay.

Laura began to show signs of acute emotional stress. She began to wet the bed, and bit her fingernails down to the quick. Sometimes she would chatter on unceasingly and other times she would hardly speak. The overall frustrations in trying to help Laura in the face of Molly's hostility began to take their toll on Diana's marriage. She felt she had no control over these most important aspects of her life. Instead she was being controlled by a woman she viewed as unstable and revengeful. Diana decided to see a therapist, who also spoke with Laura.

The therapist told Diana that she must not even offer Laura a choice of living with her and Alex because it caused too many conflicts for the child. Laura felt a strong loyalty to her mother, which was being undermined by Diana's involvement. The therapist said that Laura did need professional help and recommended a therapist who lived near Laura. Diana made the necessary arrangements for Laura to have regular visits, which she and Alex financed.

This effort made Molly even more hostile. And without her help it was impossible to get Laura to a therapist regularly. The mother began to take out on Laura what she perceived as Diana's intrusion, and the situation worsened. She wouldn't let Alex speak to his daughter on the phone. Laura was not allowed to bring any new things home and was furthermore told that she couldn't expect any Christmas gifts because there was only enough money for the younger children. Diana and Alex knew that the child-support check went into general household expenses and that Laura's needs could not adequately be met in such an overcrowded and impoverished household.

When Laura entered adolescence, Diana's concerns escalated. She began to feel a sense of panic. If something wasn't done soon Laura could end up in serious trouble. She lived in a poor section of the city where the school was known to be rough. She would soon be dating, and such things as drugs, sex, and alcohol began to loom ominously on the horizon. Diana could see Laura getting into trouble and being kicked out of the house by her mother. Then Diana and Alex would have her but by then she would probably be too damaged for real help. It seemed so unfair! Laura could have such a good life with them instead of a life of struggle.

Diana and Alex went to a lawyer and discussed instituting a custody suit. The strategy would be to have Laura examined by a school psychologist, who would surely find that she needed therapy. Since Molly had refused to take Laura to the therapist, even though Alex was paying, they could accuse her of not adequately providing for her daughter, and could argue that she was therefore an unfit mother.

Diana hesitated. She carefully thought about the process ahead of them. Molly was unreasonable and often acted irrationally. Diana knew that she and Alex could give Laura a better home environment.

But Molly was Laura's mother. As Diana put it, she was the woman who gave Laura life. The fact that Molly was poor, or that she had had four children under age six, didn't necessarily mean that she was unfit. As unreasonably as Molly had acted, Laura had never said a word against her. Diana decided she did not want to go to court to try to take Laura away. She realized that no matter how Laura's situation looked to her from the outside, a bond, a relationship, had formed between Laura and her mother that needed to be respected.

Diana's choice was to continue to try to help Laura in dealing with her life as it was. She realized that she had no control over what Laura's mother would do, but instead of becoming frustrated with a woman she found irrational, she tried to decide what *her* relationship should be with Laura. It would be, to whatever extent possible, nonthreatening. She and Alex stopped using the lawyer, and they found that Alex was better at working things out with Molly when Diana and the lawyer stayed out of it.

Instead of making such a large emotional investment in Laura, Diana concentrated more on her marriage to Alex. This did not mean that she "gave up," but she realized that although she could show concern and be available when Laura needed her, she was not Laura's mother. Laura's primary bond was with her natural mother. Diana also realized that she could not change Molly or even have much of an effect on the way she treated Laura, except in a negative way. Molly was not negotiable; she was a fact. Alex and Laura had to deal with Molly, and could probably do it better without Diana's involvement. Diana could create her own home and her own sense of family but Laura's other home and family were beyond her territory. If Laura arrives in a few years pregnant and on drugs, then Diana and Alex will deal with that at the time rather than worry about that possibility now.

This bonding between biological mother and child is a very real aspect of a stepmother's life. Stepmothers who feel as though they have done everything in their power to make a home for their stepchildren often feel hurt when their stepchildren choose to return to their natural mother. Nancy, who was described in chapter 4, could not initially understand how her stepchildren could choose to return to a mother who was unstable. Nevertheless, these children never spoke a word against their mother, and as teenagers they returned to live with her, at least for a while.

Pat, also described in chapter 4, virtually raised her three stepchildren, and now sees them fantasizing about going to live with their mother, who left them when they were very young. Pat worries that her rules—about clean rooms and homework completed before television, for example—make her seem like a tyrant in comparison to their biological mother, who is totally "laid back." She admits that one of her greatest fears is having her stepchildren go and live with their mother. After all that she has done for them it would seem so unfair, particularly since they are now at an age when they are more interesting intellectually and need less physical attention.

Pat knows, however, that she must expect it. No matter what she has done, or how much love, effort, and concern she has bestowed on her stepchildren, they have a bond with their mother, an almost visceral bond that cannot be denied.

No matter how distant or incapable the biological mother is, almost all children will try to make contact with her, primarily during their teenage years. A wonderful book written for young adults by Mary Pope Osborne, *Last One Home*, is a witty and charming description of a twelve-year-old girl who is determined to hate her stepmother, and who secretly calls her alcoholic biological mother regularly on the phone. The book describes the yearning the child has for her mother, even though that mother has been both neglectful and abusive. It also underlines her fear and resentment toward the new woman in her father's life, no matter how kind this woman has tried to be.

Children are not likely, under any circumstances, to show daily appreciation for parental love and commitment. All parents, however, including stepparents, keep going, in the belief that when the children are grown and find themselves in similar circumstances, they will at least understand what their parents were trying to do for them.

From ex-wives, though, a stepmother can rarely expect any thanks. One stepmother did receive a kind of thank-you note from her husband's ex-wife after she had raised three of her children. "It was like being dismissed as the governess— like she was saying, 'Thank you but we won't be needing you anymore.'"

Usually, stepmothers don't even get that. More than one stepmother I interviewed, having taken over the care of a woman's young children after she had left them, found the mother to be almost condescending toward her. It was as though she were saying, "I had better things to do with my life than raise children . . . but clearly that's what you wanted to do."

Once again, the stepmother must separate her actions from the ex-wife's actions. Whatever she does with her husband, her stepchildren, or her life, needs to be for her own reasons, not as a reaction to another woman. Of all the people in the world your husband's ex-wife is the last person in the world you want to depend on for satisfaction.

Sometimes the ex-wife is essentially absent, either because of death or because of severe illness. The physical absence of the ex-wife does not mean that she is really absent, however.

Walt and his daughter, Janet, had lived alone together for six years. His ex-wife suffered from severe alcoholism and lived in a nearby city. In the early years after their divorce there had been much bitterness, which involved court battles and one kidnaping. Before Janet was six her mother had become too ill to see her except for occasional visits. Janet's perception of her mother was so confused and frightening that she rarely spoke of her except with anger.

When Sylvia came into their lives, Janet was twelve. She was a pretty child, very thin with large brown eyes, just on the brink of adolescence. As pretty as she was, however, she was harsh and critical of everyone and everything. She spent most of her time alone and wore nothing but old shirts and torn jeans. She had few friends and did poorly in school.

Sylvia realized there were limits to what she could do with a child who had suffered so much. She decided that the most important thing was to give her a positive female image, a role model, since the primary female image for Janet was the shadowy figure of her mother.

They began their relationship by shopping for clothes. At first it was almost impossible. Janet would insist in store after store that there was absolutely nothing there she liked. She criticized the other girls who were shopping and said she certainly never wanted to look like them. Then, if she and Sylvia finally bought something, she would often decide she didn't like it after all and would blame Sylvia for the bad choice. Sylvia, who had raised two daughters of her own, recognized the self-defensiveness in Janet's criticisms. As she later put it, she "settled in for years of biting my tongue."

It wasn't easy but Sylvia persevered. She found these shopping trips valuable primarily for two reasons: they were especially "female," and they provided time together in which Sylvia was available to Janet. Riding in the car, eating lunch together, and walking through the stores gave Janet plenty of time to talk about things. Janet's defensive armor was too thick to be broken through easily, and it took not just months but years before Janet felt that she could trust Sylvia and be her friend. Sylvia saw their relationship as female bonding and her effort was to be a healthy female role model. It was not a mother-daughter bond but rather resembled a teacher-student or mentor-protégé relationship. It was the most comfortable way the two could establish a bond, allowing Janet to work through her confusing relationship with her natural mother.

Sylvia was very careful not to challenge Janet's loyalty to her mother, which still existed, but she tried to help her be realistic about her mother's situation. To Sylvia's credit, Janet learned to see her mother as too ill to be able to give much, and instead of being bitter and defensive, ashamed of her mother's situation, she was able to talk about her mother openly. Once, when she was visiting her mother and they were taking a walk, her mother collapsed. Janet had to call the police for help. Back in the apartment, she comforted her mother until the doctor arrived. She did not find the event overly traumatic, but accepted the fact that she was better able to take care of her mother than vice versa.

Sylvia must get some credit for this young woman's ability to deal with a tragic situation. She has given Janet a positive female role model. It has not taken the place of her mother but it has enlarged Janet's vision to include a positive image of caring. Janet has learned to be a nurturer, an occasional care-giver, and much of that was made possible through the example of Sylvia. It is important to note that Sylvia gave her stepdaughter structure, set an example, and was always available for help, but was also very careful not to challenge her loyalty to her biological mother.

Sylvia's satisfaction has not been tied to Janet's gratitude, for Janet still blames Sylvia for the wrong choices at the clothing store and fusses about her cooking. But Sylvia can see that Janet feels better about herself, has made new friends, and is much less critical and angry. Sylvia's own daughters have grown mature enough to look back on their childhood and remember the good things their mother did for them. Someday Janet may do the same, but meanwhile Sylvia enjoys the pleasure of seeing Janet growing into a lovely, pleasant young woman.

Trying to find blame, or to surpass ex-wives, or to extract gratitude from members of the stepfamily yields few truly satisfying rewards. Being true to oneself and giving freely, rather than keeping a tally sheet of obligations or injuries, is a more sensible way to live. A friend of mine always says, "Things have a way of balancing out in the end," and for my friend they always seem to. Whether it's her attitude or her lot in life, I'm not sure ... but I have a feeling it's her attitude.

8

A Mother By Any Other Name . . . Can't Tell Me What to Do!

A FRIEND WHO GREW UP IN WHITE, MIDDLE-CLASS SOUTHERN SOCIETY
tells of her introduction to a form of urban-ghetto communication. In the summer of 1961 she had just started her job as a
counselor at the *New York Herald Tribune* Fresh Air Fund
Camp in Fishkill, New York. A busload of children arrived,
hot and restless after their two-hour ride from New York City.
As she prepared to welcome her twelve-year-old female camp-
ers, one girl pushed another and snarled, "Your mother. . . ."
The pushed girl shouted, "Don't you talk about my mother!"
and within seconds the two girls were slapping, biting, and
scratching one another.

As my friend pulled the struggling girls apart, she asked,
"Your mother? What's wrong with saying 'Your mother'?"

"She can't say 'Your mother'!" the furious girl cried. "She
can say what she wants about me, but not my mother!"

My friend soon learned that "Your mother!" was a call to
battle. Behind the two words lay a wealth of slanderous
implications—that your mother was a slut or whore or even

wore combat boots. Whatever was implied in the phrase, there was overall agreement in the street language of these children that battling for your mother's name was always justified. You could stand by and maintain your young dignity if another child hit you or called you names, but once your mother was brought into the confrontation you had to fight.

The insult would have had no meaning without an accepted sense of loyalty and bonding to one's mother. This bonding is a natural extension of giving birth and begins in the first weeks of a baby's life. For the baby, it is basically preconscious and, obviously, preverbal. For this reason, the kind of initial bonding (or rejection) between mother and infant makes an indelible imprint on the individual's subconscious. The initial bond between mother and infant is primal. As one wondering young mother put it, "I carried this child under my heart for nine months."

In her book *A Country Year: Living the Questions,* Sue Hubbel writes about the feeling of a mother toward her infant:

> My baby. Mine. . . . I wanted to hold him always. My baby. . . . There was a fierceness to the love that was born the instant I saw him that startled and bewildered me. It was uncivilized, crude, unquestioning, unreasoning. I first began to understand it when, several years later, we were on a family camping trip, and during the night were awakened by an old sow bear who had wandered into our campsite with her cub. Her baby had strayed to the other side of our tent. She was frantic, fierce, angry, and would have become dangerous had not the cub waddled back to his mother of his own accord. . . . In order to become an adequate mother, I had to learn to keep the old sow bear under control. Sow-bear love is a dark, hairy sort of thing. It wants to hold, to protect; it is all emotion and conservatism.[1]

A friend's teenage son was hurt both emotionally and physically in a fight with his two best friends. She admitted that seeing his swollen face and hurt feelings was more emotionally wrenching for her than it probably was for him. She spent sleepless nights mentally venting her rage and hurt as she tossed and turned, thinking of revenge. She said, "Being a mother is hopeless! It possesses you. There is nothing you won't do to protect your child. It's shameless!"

Out of the initial, primal bond grows a complex relationship which involves a much wider range of emotions. This relationship is nevertheless still based on early physical and emotional bonding. However, this is not so for stepmothers and stepchildren.

Bruno Bettelheim, as we have seen, suggests that the psychic experience in a child's world is expressed in fairy tales. The loving, protective mother is the "real" mother, but when this mother begins to express anger or to exercise discipline, the child mentally separates the "bad" mother from the "good." They are not the same person—one is the "real" mother, the other is the stepmother.

In real stepfamily life, this duality of mothers *is* a reality. Stepmothers and stepchildren have not experienced a primal bond, and their relationship starts out at a more complex level. One stepmother candidly admitted, "I feel differently about my stepchildren. I would give my life for my own child . . . but I can't say I would for my stepchild." The relationship between mother and stepchild is not fixed instantly like the relationship between mother and newborn infant. It is a relationship that must evolve over time—and it will be different from the biological bond.

It is imperative, however, to find an "instant" name or term for a stepmother. This term can indicate the role she is expected to play regarding her stepchildren.

It's interesting to note that within families, adults usually have universal terms of identification: mother, father, aunt so and so, grandmother, grandfather. Children, however, are not called "child," "niece," or "grandchild" as a form of address. The acceptance of these adult terms, as opposed to individual names, implies relatively fixed roles that these people play within the family structure. They are, at least in part, roles of both authority and responsibility, roles that are accepted within the traditional family system.

The role of stepmother is not so clearly defined. On the one hand she is an adult, she does have responsibility and authority, and she is legally and emotionally bound to her stepchildren. The common term, however, does not seem to fit: she is not the mother. Few women would be happy being addressed simply as "stepmother." Until our language catches up with societal changes and comes up with a suitable term for the millions of stepmothers, there remain only three possibilities: mother, or some derivation of the term; a first name; or a nickname.

Although younger children may feel comfortable calling their stepmother "Mom" or "Mother," it is usually not a good idea to do more than suggest it to older children unless there is a clear signal from them that they would like to use the term.

In a previous chapter, Pat, who married a man with three very young children, was at first called "Mommie." That seemed to be what the children needed in the absence of their biological mother. When their mother moved back into the neighborhood and became more involved in their lives, the children reduced "Mommie" to "M," which stuck. They were all comfortable with this term—until her stepson went away to boarding school. He now calls her Pat, and introduces her firmly to his friends as his stepmother. Because of his age and his natural need to separate, both he and Pat are comfortable with the change. The younger children continue to call her "M," but refer to her as "Mother" in school. Although they have to explain to their teachers which mother they are referring to, this is a problem that they seem to have handled in their own way. It is interesting to note that in this family Pat has been given different names at different times by different family members, indicating both the changing nature of the stepfamily and the varying needs of family members.

Being on a first-name basis with someone usually implies equality. But in the case of stepmothers it can establish distance. Most stepmothers, especially those with older stepchildren, do settle on their first name.

My stepchildren called me Karen and, in retrospect, I believe it was the most honest approach to our situation. They had a mother, and they were not anxious for me to try to fulfill that role. Our relationship was different from their relationship with their mother. I was more of a friendly, somewhat maternal figure.

If possible, stepmothers with older children should allow them to take the lead, although it's surprising how long stepchildren can avoid calling their stepmother anything but "she" and "her." If this is the case, the stepmother could suggest that they call her something—her first name or a comfortable nickname, if possible. A stepmother need not agree to be called something she obviously dislikes, but her willingness to try variations on the term "Mother," her first name, or a nickname can set the tone for a suitable name.

It is equally important to call stepchildren by names they like. If they insist that they *hate* their given name, it can be a nice way to form a special contact if a nickname can evolve naturally. A stepmother must be especially careful, however, not to attach a nickname that the child finds in any way disparaging or uncomfortable. Names are crucial; they can be terms of affection but they can also be forms of belittlement. Names like "Munchkins" or "Petey," even if offered with affection, can drive a child into a murderous rage.

Even when everyone has settled on a comfortable term of address, there are often different last names in stepfamilies. In our home there were five Savages and my daughter Kristin, who was a Kearney. It is not surprising that she often felt "outside" the Savage circle. It is not an uncommon feeling, and statistics show that 50 percent of adoptions are within stepfamilies, partially because of the need to be like-named with a family.

This lack of tradition for stepfamilies is one of the things that make it so difficult for stepmothers to find an appropriate role to play with their stepchildren. A biological mother can both love "shamelessly, hopelessly" as my friend put it, and can express anger and exercise discipline within the accepted framework of her family. A stepmother has no traditional givens and she must find her way as she goes along—as one stepmother said, "making it up as I go."

Since a stepmother usually becomes part of a child's life only after the period of primal mother's love and acceptance, she cannot base her relationship on a previous period of physical bonding and nurturing. Although she has not experienced that relationship with the child, she is nevertheless put in the position of parenting, a role that inevitably includes disciplining.

On a recent trip to the Midwest, I overheard a woman speaking in a diner. She was distressed as she told her friend her troubles.

"I don't know what to do," she said, "Frank was out of town when she came in at 3 A.M. I was furious. She wouldn't do that if her father was home! I yelled at her, I tell you I really laid it on the line. And you know what she answered: 'You're not my mother! You can't tell me what to do!' I just wanted to hit her. I couldn't help it. I told her never to say that to me again. I'm sick of it."

There was no doubt in my mind that the woman was talking about a confrontation with her stepdaughter. I had this image of women across America, at any given hour of the day, being told, "You're not my mother. You can't tell me what to do!" It is a phrase almost every stepmother has heard.

Dr. Judith Jacobs, assistant professor of marital and family therapy at Columbia University, New York, maintains that family rules begin early, when not only the children but the family as a unit are young. These rules became almost second nature to the family and are incorporated into the family structure. A family with teenagers has had well over a decade to develop a general understanding of acceptable behavior. A stepfamily often starts the rule-making process in midstream, and there is usually a sense of urgency in establishing rules. Time works against the stepparent, however, because it takes both time and an agreement between parent and child before rules can be enforced. Biological parents have the "right" to make rules because they have nurtured the children in the early years and have contributed positively to their lives over a period of time.

In his study "A Model for Stepfamily Development," David M. Mills argues that although the stepparent should not try to approximate the role of a biological parent, particularly with teenagers, the stepparent should try to establish the *right* to function in the area of discipline. In order to achieve this right, he suggests that time be allocated to a stepparent to "bond" with a stepchild. He states,

> As the stepparent is usually starting later in the child's life, it is necessary to "artificially" re-create a period of time for nurturing without limit-setting, to allow for bonding appropriate to the age of the child.... the initial period usually requires the conscious cooperation of both parents.... For example, the stepparent will need to tie a preschooler's shoes without scolding him for misplacing them, or drive a teenager places without lecturing on dating behavior.... Initial deliberate bonding activities should be continued a year or more, depending on those involved.[2]

Mills suggests that the stepparent begin by "friending" the child before moving into a "co-management" position. Most studies suggest that this initial bonding period can take up to two years.

A stepmother has an opportunity to "friend" her stepchildren initially by physically nurturing and caring for them, i.e., by fixing their meals, washing their clothes, buying them gifts, providing transportation for them, etc. Although these activities can make a stepmother feel like a housekeeper, particularly if her efforts are met with indifference or hostility, it can nevertheless be a clear signal to her stepchildren that she wants to participate positively in their lives. A biological mother spends hours feeding, cleaning, holding, and caring for her infant without expecting gratitude, and in so doing a mutuality is set up between mother and child. A stepmother needs to look at the early stages of her relationship with stepchildren as establishing a kind of mutuality, even if their relationship is decidedly one-sided. Children in a new step-family are faced with a sense of loss of the original family, perhaps even a sense of losing the newly married biological parent, as well as possible conflicting loyalties between step-parent and biological parent. As the adult in the relationship, the stepmother must be the one to "give," at least initially. Linda Bird Francke, in her book *Growing Up Divorced*, suggests that a parent try to do something, every day, that the child could do for himself. These small daily acts can help give the child a sense of being nurtured and cared for. It can be very difficult for a stepmother to work hard to please stepchil-dren with favorite meals or to chauffeur them around to activities when her efforts are met with sullenness or anger, but her efforts can be productive in the long run. They are an investment in the future solidarity of the stepmother-stepchild relationship. This period of "giving without demanding" can be seen as an early stage in the development of that relation-ship, not as a permanent pattern. It is a way the stepmother can earn the "right" to impose discipline and eventually make reasonable demands within the family.

Ideally, there would be no need for discipline or rules while the stepparent establishes a close, nurturing relationship with the stepchild. But, in real life, the need to establish workable rules for a family spending time together usually cannot wait. According to Dr. Jacobs, it is helpful to consider the first years of stepfamily life as experimental. She advises that the family work toward clarity just for today, trying various methods for working out immediate problems and realizing that trial and error are the only methods available.

Discipline is one of the most difficult problems for a stepmother because it is often bound to feelings of anger. Although this is true for all families, in a stepfamily the separation between the expression of anger and the exercise of discipline is extremely important. Most therapists agree that feelings of anger are normal for children of divorce. Anger is also normal for someone who is rejected, or who is the object of anger, as is often the case with stepmothers. People *do* get angry and should have the right to express it. Expressing anger can have a positive effect by clearing the air, or simply by letting someone know how you feel. It is festering anger or misplaced anger that causes problems.

This festering and misplaced anger often exists in a stepfamily. It can be found in both the children and the adults. It can be particularly insidious when it has been given time to take root. It is like the burdock plant, with its spreading leaves that look deceptively like rhubarb. But burdock is a bitter plant to the taste, and the root system is deeply embedded in the soil and almost impossible to dig out. The plant puts out burrs that cling to anything that touches them, spreading the burdock farther afield. Deeply embedded anger in a family— grown out of circumstances such as divorce, fear of abandonment, mistrust, and rejection—is also very bitter; it can be very difficult to root out and can spread to whatever comes in contact with it.

Such anger can almost be expected in stepfamilies, and because it is necessary to distinguish between expressions of anger and the positive need for discipline, it is helpful to try to conceptualize how anger can manifest itself in a family situation. When the family is in stress, often one member is likely to "act out" the anxiety and in some way release the tension by causing attention to be focused on himself or herself. It can be any member of the family but usually it is a child. Children are like Geiger counters, picking up the vibrations in their home. Not able to understand or verbalize what is happening around them, they express anxiety and stress by being "difficult."

Unfortunately, many children have absorbed these conflicts and anxieties when they were too young to understand them and are therefore almost unable to deal with them. A friend told me a story that probably, at one time or another, has happened in most families. She was traveling by car with her husband. Their six-month-old daughter was sitting on her lap, playing happily, pushing her chubby fingers into her mother's eyes, pulling at her mother's hair, as her mother responded with the usual coos and nuzzles. As they were driving, my friend and her husband had a disagreement, and within minutes they were in full verbal battle. They did not shout; their voices were calm but angry. My friend distinctly remembers the reaction of her daughter. She got still, took her hands away from her mother's face, and as the parents continued in their quiet, bitter discussion she became rigid. The child could feel the anger between her parents. She effectively absorbed it into her little mind and body. This, of course, does not mean any child who overhears a family argument is damaged for life, but it does indicate that children who have experienced divorce have certainly received more than their share of psychic blows.

Dr. Patricia Papernow maintains that anger and the resulting disruptive behavior among family members is normal in a stepfamily. Children whose families have been disrupted can be expected to feel anger. Rarely, however, is a child intellectually sophisticated enough to recognize this anger for what it is and from where it comes. He or she more often acts out by being disruptive, sullen, or withdrawn. In an ideal world we would all understand the real source of our anger and focus it. This is not an ideal world, however, and it is unrealistic to expect a child to always express anger in an "acceptable" way.

There are two positive steps a stepmother can take when dealing with a particularly difficult stepchild. One is to try to recognize when a child clearly needs professional help. Another is to establish what is and is not acceptable behavior and to try, through caring and discipline, to achieve harmony.

Although it is neither practical nor productive to race off to the therapist's office when a child throws temper tantrums or is caught smoking in his or her room, a consistent pattern of anger, hostility, or deviant behavior may well indicate that professional help is needed. The "biggies" that we all worry about in teenagers—running away, drug or alcohol abuse, signs of anorexia, or hostile social acts—are usually signs of trouble. In younger children, persistent bodily misfunctions, withdrawal, or constant hostility to parents or other children may mean that the child has become a receptacle for the anger and stress around him or her.

Most expressions of anger and "normal" acting out, however, must be dealt with on a day-by-day basis within the stepfamily, and this calls for some method of discipline. Discipline is necessary for two reasons: to maintain stability in a household, and to teach a youngster what is and is not acceptable. Conscientious discipline takes time, energy, and commitment. The common quote "Spare the rod and spoil the child" actually reads, in Proverbs, "He that spareth his rod hateth his son; but he that loveth him chasteneth him betimes." The full quote is much more humane than the cliché, and to "chasten betimes" is not the same concept as coming down hard, again and again, with the rod (even metaphorically) on an erring child. The definition of chasten in *Webster's New World Dictionary* reads; "1: to punish in order to correct or make better 2: to restrain from excess; subdue 3: to make purer in style; refine."

In her book *The Successful Stepparent,* Helen Thompson gives some worthwhile suggestions on establishing overall discipline goals. Children should be punished for their acts but not for their feelings; they have a right to be angry but must learn to express their anger appropriately. Young children should be punished quickly—and it should be over fast. Punishment should be intended to help a child develop emotional control, to relieve him or her of a burden of guilt, and even to give him or her a chance to feel angry.[3]

Correct discipline should always have an ulterior motive. It should be thought out and planned, and conscientiously followed through to a conclusion. The ultimate aim should be to "make better" or in some cases to subdue, or even to refine behavior. In order for discipline to be effective in this way, there must be an overall goal for the parents. This goal should include not only how the parents hope the members of the family will relate to one another, but also a clarification of the stepparent-stepchild relationship. This may mean that the stepparent hopes to eventually "parent" the stepchild, or it could mean that the stepparent hopes, rather, to establish a comfortable, friendly, but distant relationship. A stepparent will participate in disciplining stepchildren differently depending on the ultimate aim. This aim should be understood by both parents, so before a stepmother can successfully discipline or refrain from disciplining, she and her husband must agree on certain goals.

If a stepmother intends to participate in the disciplining of her stepchildren, it is vital that she be supported by her husband, the children's biological father. Many stepmothers complain that their husbands are lax about discipline. My own husband, Lee, was referred to as "Dr. Yes" by all of our children. Particularly with his own children, whom he did not live with, he was reluctant to do anything to spoil the time they had together. Even though a father does not want to be the bad guy and is struggling with his own personal feelings of loss or guilt regarding his children, he must be fair to his wife. Without his support and agreement on methods of discipline, it is almost impossible for the stepmother to exercise positive discipline toward her stepchildren. Although working through methods of discipline is difficult in the short run, inability or refusal to do so results in long-term problems for everyone in the family.

The first and most vital step, therefore, is to establish the goals you hope to reach and a style of discipline that is both realistic and comfortable for both parents. This can be one of the hardest arrangements to make. Unlike a biological family, a stepfamily is made up of individuals who are different in a multitude of ways: they are different ages, have different histories and different loyalties. Most stepchildren are members of two households, which invariably have different sets of rules. In order to establish goals for the stepfamily a couple needs to keep these differences in mind, and needs to work to establish goals that are fitted to the individual needs of family members.

In stepfamilies, parents have usually developed their own style of disciplining in their previous marriage. It is hard to change this style, even if the circumstances have changed. A parent who has been generally relaxed and patient cannot suddenly become stern and forceful. A parent who is by nature a firm disciplinarian cannot totally reverse his or her nature.

Couples tend to work toward a balance between themselves, but this balance usually evolves over time. The couple who have come together to form the stepfamily are usually still in the early stages of adjusting to each other's behavior and methods of communicating. Nevertheless, when they become "joint parents" of their two families there is a need to create instant roles, which may or may not "fit." Making rules or exercising discipline cannot work if the parents are uncomfortable in their role.

Occasionally parents cannot agree on certain rules. According to David Mills, "Because of the unique nature of the stepfamily, if parent and stepparent cannot find agreement on a given rule, by default it must go the biological parent's way. The reason is simply that the children will not obey any rules the biological parent does not agree with."[4]

Even if parents are not always in agreement, or if the particular styles of discipline differ between parents, if the overall goals are the same and the parents are supportive of each other's methods and convictions, then eventually the stepfamily will function satisfactorily. It is important to keep in mind, however, that establishing comfortable rules and methods of discipline will take time, and that some mistakes will be inevitable.

A stepmother should try to keep her eye on the long-term goal and then live each day the best way she can. A true form of child abuse is neglect, and fair discipline is the opposite of neglect. It is evidence of caring, of attention, of self-respect, and a desire for the good of the child.

9

Adolescence: A Topic Unto Itself

MOST FAMILY THERAPISTS MAINTAIN THAT BEHAVIOR THAT WOULD indicate major emotional problems in adults is perfectly normal in adolescents. Like the body used to create the monster in Mel Brooks's comedy film *Young Frankenstein*, each adolescent could be named "Abby Normal." An average teenager is alternately a hysterical personality disorder, a delightful companion, an antisocial personality, an inquisitive human being, and a two-year-old, all rolled into one bundle of energy. Any household with an adolescent is potentially a household in a state of crisis. Adolescence is perhaps nature's way of preparing parents to tolerate and even welcome the empty nest.

Recently, at a cocktail party, a woman whose only child was twelve said that she had heard such frightening things about teenage boys but that she couldn't imagine her own son acting up in such ways. "Well, just brace yourself," a woman whose daughters had already passed through that stage replied. On the couch, her twenty-two-year-old daughter sat

115

talking to a friend, the picture of poise and youthful beauty. "You'll make it through ... but sometimes you won't believe you will."

Adolescence is being born again for the child and going through labor again for the parent. The adolescent is being reborn into a new world of adult feelings, possibilities, and problems. The parents "labor" to help him or her through, but when it is all over and they have a healthy adult before them, the pain and burden of that labor is forgotten in the joy of that human being. Many parents who told tales of woe during their children's adolescence find it hard to remember what the fuss was all about when their children mature into interesting and healthy adults.

One of the reasons that adolescence is such a volatile period in family life is that families with adolescents are often in the throes of three major life crises at the same time. The children are teenagers—nice children who have overnight turned into strangers who criticize your every move, dress strangely, listen to tribal music at an unbearable pitch, and insist on thinking for themselves, even when they have no experience on which to base their decisions. The parents are often in their late thirties or forties, halfway through their own lives, acutely conscious of what they have accomplished and what they have not. Almost everyone experiences some form of mid-life crisis and the accompanying reevaluation of goals and priorities can shake the family to its foundations. Thirdly, the grandparents are probably entering old age. Parents are seeing their own parents become childlike and dependent just when their teenagers are becoming adult and independent. The death of parents signals that you are up next; the care of aging parents often puts a strain on the family. At no other time does the family have to face so much stress at one time.

Stepfamilies tend to blame everything that goes on in the family on the fact that they are living in a stepfamily. Normal developmental problems, stages that every family experiences along the way, are seen as stepfamily problems. Acting-out adolescents are perceived to be rebelling against the fact that their mother and father live in different houses. Guilty parents, overly aware that divorce and remarriage have displaced their children, shoulder the blame for behavior that is often just the normal, predictable rebellion of adolescents. Certainly a divorce that occurs when the children in the family are in their teens is usually more disruptive for them than one that occurs either earlier or later, since the major task of adolescence is separation and it is hard to separate from a family that suddenly separates from you. Teenagers need a stable family to break away from, one that can tolerate their unpredictable mood changes without taking them too personally. Adults in the throes of a divorce are often too insecure themselves to provide stability for their children. Kids sometimes end up feeling they have to be there for their parents instead of their parents being there for them. However, stepfamily members need to be aware that the majority of the problems that arise in a stepfamily with teenagers would be going on even if the family were not a stepfamily. These problems *are* going on in every family that finds itself at that particular stage in the family life cycle.

Most parents are unprepared for their children's adolescence, and stepparents are no exception. A clear understanding of what to expect during this difficult time can make a tremendous difference in how the family weathers this particular storm. Early adolescence is the most difficult time of life, and this critical period of growth and change is more painful and hazardous to negotiate today then it has ever been before. The omnipresence of drugs, sexual pressures, the gloomy state of the world, and a divorce rate of almost 50 percent all combine to provide adult temptations to teenagers who are often not receiving adequate guidance from the adults in their lives. In his article "Puberty and Parents," Dr. Bruce Baldwin, a practicing psychologist who heads Direction Dynamics in Wilmington, North Carolina, describes the stages of adolescence.[1] He explains what teenagers are experiencing and also examines the emotions aroused in parents as their children move through these stages.

Dr. Baldwin points out that parents regularly experience three apprehensions when their children reach puberty:

1. My adolescent will do the same things I did when I was young.

Almost all of us take chances when we are teenagers, and the thought of our children doing the same foolish things that we did is frightening. Erma Bombeck recently commented wryly on how our kids delight in telling us what they got away with when it is too late to do anything about it.

2. The world is more dangerous now than it was when I was young.

True. Not only is the world more dangerous, certain accepted guidelines are no longer prevalent. A friend remarked that growing up in the fifties was like walking through a snowfield. Before her were nice big footprints and if she just put her feet in those footprints, then she believed everything would work out. Now, the snowfield has turned into an avalanche, with masses of stone and gravel where any step could mean disaster.

3. My child now has a private life, which I can't control anymore.

Looking after children is fairly easy when they are small but our sense of being in control is constantly eroded by the burgeoning independence and accompanying secrecy of teenagers. The title of the book by Robert Paul Smith, *Where Did You Go? Out. What Did You Do? Nothing,* epitomizes the typical adolescent response to parental curiosity. Parents find themselves searching rooms and reading diaries, behavior that shames them and that they would not believe themselves capable of under any other circumstances.

The terrifying news of drug addiction, teenage murders, and sexual promiscuity often makes parents almost paranoid. One mother tells of finding a can of baking powder in her thirteen-year-old son's bedroom. Although she was vague about the process of "cutting" cocaine, she was convinced that baking powder was used. First she took the baking powder away but then decided to put it back and see if she could catch him using it. She did. One afternoon as she passed his room she saw him hunched over with the can of baking powder in his hand. She decided to confront him, only to see that he was shaking it between his toes, thinking that it might cure his athlete's foot.

She felt silly and also ashamed. She had had no real reason to assume he was using cocaine, but the news media had put her in a state of anxiety and suspicion.

Dr. Baldwin divides adolescence into three basic stages spanning almost twenty years. This extended time for adolescent development is a relatively new phenomena in our society. It is generally accepted that "childhood" is over earlier today than it used to be through the child's wider exposure to the adult world, and it is extended on the other side by longer periods of education and different societal expectations for the young adult. A man's whose eighteen-year-old son was being difficult said, "I'm giving Johnny until he's thirty to shape up ... but not a year more!" The man was making a joke, but he was probably closer to the truth than he realized.

Dr. Baldwin divides the stages of adolescence into three age spans.

1. Early adolescence (the rise of tribal loyalties) ages ten to seventeen.

During this stage the peer group becomes all-important as the child struggles to begin the process of separation. Fanatic loyalty to the group, and rigid adherence to its dress and behavior codes and other powerfully-enforced inclusion criteria, rule adolescents' lives. They push parents away and resist advice, testing parental limits to the edges of parental tolerance. Undergoing the physical changes of puberty, they are getting used to their new bodies, new urges, and new responsibilities while they are still barely out of childhood. This stage can begin in the fifth or sixth grade. The future is far away; the child lives in the present, and his or her thoughts about direction in life are naive and unrealistic.

2. Middle adolescence: ages eighteen to twenty-four.

Beginning in late high school, adolescents begin to realize that *real life* is about to begin, ready or not. They face the decision of making a choice between college and work, and begin to test themselves in the world, often learning a few painful lessons about their capacities and abilities. Still more or less under the parental roof but forced to make most decisions on their own, they feel a combination of fear and excitement. The realization sinks in that it's really up to them. Middle adolescents are less defensive with parents, more preoccupied with their own struggle to find themselves than actively rebellious. Still, fights are apt to erupt over choices of life-style, choice of career, and degree of responsibility. Parents find themselves ready to let go, but they want to make sure they have taught all the right lessons to enable their children to negotiate the tricky passage to adulthood. The old peer group still has some importance but new friendships made at college and at work are deeper. One-to-one relationships instead of group relationships take precedence. Opposite-sex relationships become more important. Facing the necessity of making a living, young people get more realistic about opportunities and goals.

3. Late adolescence: ages twenty-four to thirty.

By their mid-twenties, most late adolescents are on their own, and fairly free from protective parental involvement. This process is sometimes retarded in areas where high rents force young adults to live at home for financial reasons. Boomerang children, those who come back home again after leaving the nest, have a difficult time completing the process of separation while they are still under the same roof with their parents. This is one place where being a stepfamily works to advantage: moving in with another parent, a family you didn't grow up with, usually allows you more freedom than going back home. The very openness of the stepfamily system tends to encourage adolescent growth and separation. There are also more role models for the adolescent to choose from.

Late adolescents are usually working, which gives them practical experience in the use of their abilities. They are learning how to manage money, do laundry, and prepare their own meals. Relationships with parents are usually much better and are friendlier and closer than before. One of the tasks of adolescence, "the death of parent as hero," has been accomplished. Late adolescents see their parents as people and often discover that they like them. Love relationships are more grown-up and tend to preoccupy every waking moment that is not devoted to the job. As late adolescents settle down, marriage begins to appear desirable. Work goals are more and more important. The good life beckons.

Of these stages, early adolescence is the most difficult, both for parents and for children. Young teenagers are still very vulnerable and have little experience to protect themselves from painful and dangerous mistakes. It helps to realize that your children are just doing what they are supposed to be doing at this stage of the game and that they have not gone off the track entirely or turned into monsters. Comparing notes with other parents of adolescents and having a sense of humor and proportion help parents through this period. Above all, the ability not to take adolescent anger, moodiness, and rebelliousness personally will enable you to stay adult and not descend into adolescence yourself.

Dr. Baldwin discusses the most common early-adolescent attitudes that may make life difficult for parents but are perfectly normal for kids. While teenagers reject parental standards, there is an absolute need to conform to the standards of their peer group. Their acceptance in this peer group is linked to having certain externals: the right friends, clothes, or teenage-fad items. Parents are badgered to finance certain status items seen as necessary for success with a chosen peer group.

Teenage personal grooming can take an inordinate amount of time, and any small physical imperfection, from the size of a nose to a pimple, can seem catastrophic. These externals are very important to the child's self-image, and it is hard to convince young adolescents that the cut of their jeans or the way their sneakers are tied won't make that much difference. It will. Teenagers are acutely aware of how they look and acutely aware of how others look. Friendships during this period are unstable and can flounder on such seemingly small things as "looking like a dufus" or saying the wrong thing. Teens can be incredibly insensitive to one another. Hurtful teasing and gossip are part of daily life for most adolescents.

Although teenagers tend to be very social within their peer group, they withdraw from family. They need to be alone when they are at home and they are no longer as interested in participating in family activities as they were when they were children. They particularly dislike being questioned by adults, and attempts by parents to give helpful advice are met with attitudes of boredom or hostility.

Teens live in the present. Discussing the future with early adolescents is an exercise in futility. Their future is submerged in a rich fantasy life where everything is possible. . . . They see themselves as famous rock stars, Olympic champions, beautiful models, or wealthy executives.

Yet, with all these impractical qualities of the teen years, adolescents still need and demand a certain amount of independence. They want to make their own decisions by themselves and want to break rules they see as circumventing their desires. They have "almost" adult bodies and want to experiment with such adult things as sex, drugs, and tobacco. All this is *normal*.

Teenagers aren't the only ones who go through predictable stages. Parents of teenagers find that they have many feelings in common. A child's growing up forces parents to grow up as well. Learning to deal with one's own reactions to a teenager often changes a parent forever. Some of the emotions aroused are:

1. Fear.

Teenagers start to behave in potentially dangerous ways just when they stop telling us what they are doing. Every parent knows the feeling of lying awake at night, waiting for the teenager to come home, imagining all the things that may have gone wrong . . . from drug use to car wrecks. Allowing the teenager enough freedom and independence to make his or her own decisions (and mistakes) takes a lot of parental maturity. Some families find themselves erecting stringent rules as a bulwark against disaster, only to find that they have not left enough room for their child to grow up.

2. Helplessness.

When children were little you could always kiss it and make it well. Teenagers have lost the belief that adults can help. They don't even think adults know what they are talking about. They forget that we were there once—and we often forget, too. It is a help for us to remember the dramas of our own adolescent experiences, and that we survived them. It helps blunt the pain of not being able to help our children through their pain now.

3. Frustration.

The adolescent need to separate from the family usually shows itself by the children's pushing against parental rules and limits and confronting parents about almost everything. The fact that this is normal and even desirable—it shows that your teenagers are thinking for themselves—is not much help to the adult, who predictably becomes angry, threatened, stressed, and exhausted.

4. A sense of loss.

Very often our sense of ourselves as adults is tied up in our vision of ourselves as parents. We have been parents for most of our adult lives. Taking care of someone has become a way of life. Suddenly, with the children gone, we are face to face with each other, and many couples find themselves fearful of being alone together. The children may have served as an emotional defense against the emptiness of the marriage, and many divorces occur at this time. Stepparents are not usually in this category because they married when they were older and already had children, and the adult couple usually want to be alone together. In second marriages, mates are often chosen more wisely than in first ones because both partners have more maturity and are able to use their experience to avoid mistakes. Whereas in first marriages the children's leaving home may cause trouble in the marriage, in second marriages the chief problems have often *been* the children. Their departure can leave the couple feeling that the chief stress in their marriage is now gone. When asked why their second marriages had broken up, 80 percent of the stepparents surveyed cited the children as their biggest problem. Along with the sense of impending loss, then, may also come fantasies of how peaceful life will be without the teenager in the house.

5. Hurt feelings.

Anyone raising children and expecting gratitude is making a fundamental mistake. Kids may end up being grateful to their parents when they have safely traversed the stages of adolescence and have emerged on the other side, becoming able to see their parents as people, but average teenagers regard their parents as hopeless. They may admit to a sneaking fondness for them but they wouldn't want to show it. Disgusted looks and sighs greet most parental comments. One mother tells the story of starting out on a long trip with her young teenage sons in the backseat of the car.

"This is going to be a wonderful family trip," she announced. "I hope we can all remain cheerful and really enjoy each other!"

"OK," the boys agreed. "But you have to promise one thing, Mom."

"Of course. What is it?"

"*DON'T KISS US!*"

It takes a thick skin to bear being made fun of by your own child, and sometimes a teenager's criticism can be particularly hurtful—especially if it cuts close to the bone. Often your child has the gift of seeing you as others see you and he or she is more than willing to share that gift with you, usually to your disadvantage. It can be helpful, although painful, to listen to that caustic teenager because there is probably at least a grain of truth in his or her criticism. Your teenager may be one of the few people who will observe you so closely and critically.

A parent's biggest job during this period is to remain calm and to remember that the kids will eventually grow up into rational human beings. After all, you did. Your example is the most important thing you ever give to your children. It weighs much more heavily than what you say. You need to have gotten yourself together by the time your children reach adolescence because this period will require every ounce of your maturity. Liking your life, finding meaning in it and in your relationships, and genuinely liking as well as loving your adolescent is the goal.

Parents need to be strong, sticking to their convictions in the face of a questioning and often critical audience. They need to be consistent, making decisions about reasonable and acceptable behavior and enforcing these decisions. Just because teenagers push so hard against boundaries doesn't mean they don't need them. Fair boundaries make kids feel safe and cared for. If nobody cares whether or not you come home at a reasonable hour at night, you are much more likely not to care yourself.

The best way for families to formulate rules for adolescents is for the parents and the kids to sit down together and come up with a set of rules that both feel they can live with. Kids are much less likely to violate rules that they themselves have helped create. Flexibility is also important: what seems to be a reasonable rule for a fourteen-year-old needs modification by the time he or she is sixteen.

Most important, be aware that all behavior *means* something. Try to understand what is beneath the adolescent's mood swings and rebellions by remembering what a hard time this is, and what an immense job it is to get through it. Be ready to respond to the emotional needs the child may not be able to articulate.

Teenagers can be very confusing, however. Beverly's stepdaughter, Judy, asked to come and live with her father, Charles, when she was fifteen. Beverly had always found Judy delightful, even though she had only seen her during vacation visits. She thought Judy and her own daughter, Tina, who was four, would establish a close bond.

Judy came, enrolled in the local school, and seemed anxious to please. She volunteered to baby-sit and to take Tina with her on outings. She raved about how happy she was in school as she left each morning with her books. Beverly enjoyed more freedom than she had before Judy came, and felt comfortable leaving Tina with her. Then Tina began to relate what she and Beverly did together. Instead of taking a bus to the movies, Tina and Judy were being picked up by teenage boys and racing around town. Evenings Beverly thought Tina and Judy were sitting quietly at home were spent entertaining a wide range of young people. When Beverly checked the liquor supply, the gin bottle was filled with water and the bourbon bottle was filled with tea.

Then the school called. Judy had not attended school in three weeks. Naturally Beverly was furious. Her first instinct was to send Judy back home to her mother but her husband intervened. He said, "You have to understand that this Judy that we see is like an aberration. She's not the 'real' Judy— she's a teenager! We have to remember the delightful child she was before . . . and I know she will become that again. It's like having a wart or something that will eventually go away."

When the parents talked to Judy they found that she was terrified of school and meeting new people. It had been easier for her to fall in with the kids who hung out at the mall—they were much less threatening to her. She needed friendship and was willing to do anything to get it, including inviting kids over to drink.

Once they understood what problems Judy faced, Beverly and Charles were able to help her. They also realized that she was not ready to take on the responsibility of a young child and no longer asked her to baby-sit.

Beverly can look back now and see that Charles was correct. Judy had been a delightful child and she did become a delightful adult . . . but while she was a teenager, she was a trial.

Kids need to know that you are on their side no matter what. Adolescents can be wonderful and it's thrilling when they begin to teach you things. The more you feel proud of your kids the prouder they will be able to feel about themselves.

Adolescents who live in stepfamilies go through all these stages, as do their parents. Understanding what is normal and predictable behavior during this period is often a great help to both. There are, however, some things that tend to be different because the family involved is a stepfamily.

Rules are important during the teenage years because adolescent enthusiasm and experimentation need some containment. It is often easier for parents to agree on rules than it is for parent and stepparent. Stepparents find themselves being stricter in most cases because that little extra, indulgent edge that a parent has is missing. What a parent can tolerate and what a stepparent can tolerate are often two different things. It is often easy to put down teenagers for their behavior—they almost seem to invite it. But stepparents need to watch themselves, making sure they aren't just trying to "get" the adolescent. Each parent needs to be conscious of the difference, and respectful of it.

Going back and forth between two households, each containing a parent and perhaps a stepparent, can mean that the adolescent is exposed to different rules and behavioral standards. If one household is indulgent and the other strict, it can be very confusing. Especially during these adolescent years it is helpful if the two households can come to some basis of agreement on how to deal with rules and transgressions. It is more fruitful, when a rule is broken, to sit down with a teenager and figure out what was going on, why it happened, and how it can be avoided in the future than it is to impose a punishment arbitrarily, which can increase the teenager's sense of not being understood. Children want to get along with their parents and as long as the parent doesn't set up an adversarial situation most kids will be cooperative. Frightened parents come on too strong, and trust can easily be eroded. Communication, honesty, and goodwill are the most important aids in talking with adolescents.

In a biological family teenagers are stuck with their families. In a stepfamily situation there is often another family where they can live if things don't work out at home. There are times when a move from one parent's household to the other's may be a good idea. Adolescents sometimes find that their father tolerates their push toward separation better than their mother. This is especially true if the mother has not remarried and has become overly dependent on the children. If a situation with one parent becomes untenable (and passions can run high during these years), it is helpful to have another home to go to, even if only for a cooling-off period. However, it is important to assess the needs of the situation. Teenagers should not be allowed to play one parent off against the other, running back and forth because a parent tries to impose reasonable limits on their behavior. Equally important, parents should *never* threaten to send children off to live with another parent as a way of coercing them into behaving. Feeling unwanted at home is a terrible feeling. Teenagers may believe these threats and their sense of security may be seriously eroded. A move from one household to another needs to be carefully and cooperatively thought out by everyone, including the stepparents. Having a teenager move suddenly into your house will radically change the family, and everyone living in that family deserves to have a say in the decision.

For an adolescent, it may feel safer to indulge in real, flamboyant adolescent behavior with a parent than with a stepparent. The security children feel with a parent, the sense that he or she will love them no matter what, enables kids to let themselves rebel without being too afraid of rejection. With a stepparent, the feeling is slightly different. The parental bond isn't there—a stepparent just might reject them if they behave too badly. Also, some adolescents use being a teenager as an excuse to play the good old game of "get the stepparent."

However, there are some very positive things about being an adolescent in a stepfamily. A teenager has more adult role models to observe and learn from, and a stepparent can fill a role in a teenager's life as a concerned, interested, but slightly removed friend. It is often easier to talk to a stepparent about such difficult topics as sex and drugs than to a parent. Also, the flexibility kids learn from life in a stepfamily is very good training for real life. Being able to get along with many different people is a skill that serves anyone in good stead.

In our family, my stepdaughter Kate moved in with us when she was sixteen and stayed until she was nineteen. She and her mother were having a difficult time, and although the move turned out to be a good one for us, it was not done with the careful planning that I now realize is essential.

Kate called up one day and said, "Dad, I can't live here anymore. Come and get me." Like a knight in shining armor, Lee rushed to the rescue. The result was a court battle and years of hard feelings between us and Lee's ex-wife, who felt, quite correctly, that she should have been consulted before such a radical change was undertaken.

Kate was as wonderful with us as she had been difficult with her mother. Her need for rebellion seemed to vanish with the change of family. I had been somewhat apprehensive about how she would fit into the family on a full-time basis, but she seemed to feel at home right away and for the most part was a definite asset rather than a problem. She is the stepchild I have been closest to, largely because she did live with us for a longer period than Pete and Willy did. Our relationship has continued to be a pleasure, full of mutual respect, admiration, and love. If I had it to do over again, however, I would be more thoughtful about such a radical move. Lee, his ex-wife, and I should have discussed the problems between Kate and her mother and assessed the possible solutions rather than rushing into anything. I think that Lee and I got sidetracked into trying to win the who-is-the-better-parent sweepstakes (another typical stepfamily game) rather than looking at what was best for everyone involved. Luckily, it turned out that the move was a good thing for Kate and for us, and our present warm relationship is a result.

One stepmother found that having her stepdaughter move back in with her biological mother made stepparenting much easier than she had ever expected. When Barbara and Steve married, his six-year-old daughter Pam lived with them. Although Barbara invested much time and emotion in Pam and was hurt when she decided to move to the distant city where her mother lived, Barbara soon realized that she was getting the best of the deal. Pam's normal adolescent anger and rebellion were focused on her biological mother, and the summers she spent with Barbara and Steve enabled Pam and Barbara to build a friendship out of their earlier stepmother-stepdaughter relationship. Barbara found that although she cared for Pam, her emotional investment was different from that of a biological parent, and she was able to accept Pam's teenage behavior without feeling personally threatened.

Stepfamilies tend to have more crises than other types of families; families with adolescents tend to have more crises than other types of families. It follows that stepfamilies with adolescents are experiencing two sorts of stress, step-stress and teen-stress, at the same time. If they are not adequately prepared they can find themselves overwhelmed. It is essential for parents and stepparents to learn what the difference is between normal adolescent turmoil and real, out-of-control distress. Because stepfamilies have their own inherent problems, teenagers sometimes have a harder time separating from them. Being aware of all these factors, neither overreacting nor underreacting, and holding adolescents in a loose but firm family embrace, parents and stepparents can help their children negotiate this stormy passage.

10

Sex and Violence

LOST IN THE LAND OF NO TABOOS

LIFE BEGINS IN THE DARK, WARM, ALL-ENCOMPASSING SECURITY OF THE
womb. The process of birth is the first step in the normal
separation of mother and infant. Birth involves the infant's
own push toward freedom and light combined with the mother's push to bring the baby forth from her body. At first a
child is swaddled in blankets and gowns which give it the same
sense of closeness as the womb, but it soon pushes against this
confinement and wants the space and freedom to wave and
kick. As the child begins to crawl and then walk, there is still
a need to be held and caressed. The arms and lap of the parent
give a sense of security. Although the process of development
in a child is accompanied by a diminishing need for such close
physical attachment to the parent, the need for physical
contact does not disappear. Young children begin to develop
closeness with other children and with toys or pets. As
interaction with peers develops, the child finds outlets for this
physical need in activities such as roughhousing, wrestling, or

131

playing intimate touching games with friends. As sexual awareness grows, children become increasingly interested in their own and others' bodies. They play doctor or mommie-and-daddy games. As they approach adolescence these needs are more directly focused on peers, with experimental efforts of affection that are derived as often from curiosity as from a true sense of caring. Ultimately the individual finds a mate with whom he or she can express full sexual love, and the process begins again.

This simplified outline of human sexual development does not begin to encompass the complexities and variations that exist in human society. If one considers, however, the journey from the warm security of the womb to the sexuality of the adult, it is clear that parents play an essential role in the sexual development of their children. Initially, the parents' physical connection to the child forms a basis for later physical relationships. A parent's physical closeness gives warmth, steadiness, something that is nonthreatening. In his book *Touching: The Human Significance of the Skin*, Ashley Montagu says:

> The mother's holding and cuddling of the child plays a very effective and important part in its subsequent sexual development. A mother who loves her child enfolds it. She draws the child to her in a close embrace and, male or female, this is what as adults they will later want and be able to do to anyone they love. Children who have been inadequately held and fondled will suffer, as adolescents and adults, from an affect-hunger for such attention.[1]

This early physical bonding progressively lessens as the child develops, but as the child moves farther away from the parent the sense of security and trust established in infancy and maintained throughout childhood is essential for the mental health of the individual. If at any stage parental affection takes on sexual overtones, this sense of security and trust is destroyed. A closeness that should be warm and secure becomes horrible and sometimes violent when incest occurs.

The incest taboo has been observed in almost all societies since recorded history. A taboo, as opposed to a law, is something that is forbidden by tradition and convention. Although incest can also be illegal, it is the taboo, so deeply ingrained in our society, that acts as the stronger deterrent, since the legal system does not normally have access to the inner dynamics of a family. Although the argument has been made that the incest taboo exists for primarily biological reasons—i.e., interfamily conception would eventually weaken a society to the point of extinction—there are also deep psychological reasons why parents are forbidden to have sexual relations with their children. A sexual relationship is different from the physical expressions of affection between parent and child in that parental affection is "nondirective." Caressing, soothing, and holding a child is not precursory to something else. Unlike sexual expressions, parental affection is not building toward an ultimate act of intimacy. It is, in a sense, passive. Much parental holding ends with the child falling peacefully asleep. It is this quality that makes it secure, nonthreatening. Consider the difference between this form of contact and the essentially moving, probing, and arousing actions of sexual activity. Rather than giving security, un-wanted sexual advances are a harsh intrusion on the psyche of the individual.

Although a child may be curious about or enjoy his or her own body, children generally find anything overtly sexual in adults frightening. Freudian psychologists maintain that sex must be experienced by the child as disgusting as long as his or her sexual longings are attached to the opposite-sex parent, because such a negative attitude toward sex helps keep the incest taboo secure. Only when a child is at an age to direct his or her sexual feelings toward a partner of a more suitable age will sex become less fearsome. It is often during this transition period, a time when the child has not totally released his or her sexual longings toward a parent but is mature enough to express sexual feeling, that the incest taboo is broken. Although the child must always be considered the victim in such cases, the dynamics of parent-child relationships during this period can be very complicated.

Incest between father, or father figure, and daughter is the most frequently broken of the incest taboos. To better understand the complex sexual relationship between a father and daughter, it is informative to return once again to one of our oldest forms of literature, the fairy tale. "The Beauty and the Beast" and "The Frog Prince" are tales told in varying forms in many cultures. In "The Frog Prince" a girl agrees to bring the frog to her table and into her bed when he returns her "golden ball" (her favorite plaything) from a deep well. In this and other fairy tales like it, the frog (or beast) has been turned into a disgusting creature by a female sorceress or witch, and it is the girl's *father* who insists that she keep her promise, which results in transforming the vile creature into a prince. If the frog or beast is an image of sexuality, it is at first presented as a loathsome, slimy thing. This frightening image is the result of a female action, perhaps representing the protection a mother tries to give her daughter by enforcing the child's wariness of sexual matters. It is only after the girl overcomes her disgust and kisses the frog, takes it into her bed, or performs some other act with sexual overtones that the frog changes into a charming prince. The father insists that the daughter face the reality of sexuality and in so doing helps her become an adult. The symbolic role of the father in contemporary weddings is in keeping with the old fairy tales. A father brings his daughter, dressed in virginal white, to the groom and "gives" her to him.

These customs and fairy tales show how important and complex the role between father and daughter can be. A father does not play a passive role in the sexual maturing of his daughter; their relationship throughout her childhood is a key factor in determining her ability to develop a healthy sexual relationship as an adult. Early bonding with a father plus a continued sense of trust and security can eventually enable a female to establish a satisfying sexual life.

This transition from the early, highly physical expressions of love between father and daughter to the adult forms of mutual affection between them can be a rocky road for both, however. During it, the father sees his daughter developing sexually, and mixed with his awareness of her as a woman rather than a child is the strong protective urge of the father. It is when the sexual feelings of the father are stronger than his "fathering" or protective feelings that incest can occur. The concept of incest between father and daughter is so disturbing because the child expects and needs nonthreatening security from a man who violates her instead. It is the ultimate breach of trust.

Incest breeds violence. We hear horrifying statistics about sexual abuse in families. Recently, in Washington, D.C., a girl who committed suicide left a notebook detailing sexual abuse by her adoptive father. And in New York State, a young woman was accused of hiring a friend to kill her father because of his sexual demands on her.

The statistical evidence of sexual abuse in the family, and the attention being given to this phenomenon in the media, exposes an extreme form of sexual tension that can exist in families. These cases of sexual abuse stand in direct opposition to our image of a "normal happy family," but between these two extremes lies a vast gray area in which most families, and particularly stepfamilies, are trying to find their way. Many fathers can experience some kind of sexual attraction for their daughters, but the strong taboo coupled with a deep sense of responsibility and parental love keeps this attraction well submerged.

For a stepfather, however, the situation is different. Few stepfathers have had the opportunity to hold their stepdaughter as an infant and to form any preverbal bond with her. The stepfather's relationship with the stepdaughter almost always begins while she is in the process of moving away from such intimate contact, even though she may still express a need for parental intimacy. He also does not have the strong biological tie with his stepdaughter that makes the protective urge so strong. Nevertheless, a stepfather is often expected to play a fathering role. He is, after all, a helpmate to her mother, and his stepdaughter's very proximity to and involvement in his life demand that he participate in her development in some ways. As a father figure, the stepfather has a relationship with his stepdaughter that can be difficult not only for him but for the daughter and her mother as well.

These problems are most clearly manifested when a girl is pubescent or older, but they can also exist with younger children. Although a young child may love to be held and caressed by a stepparent, the stepfather needs to be careful not to inadvertently cross a physical barrier that would make the child feel threatened.

The relaxed sexual attitudes that were common during and after the liberation movements of the sixties and seventies can also pose particular problems in the stepfamily.

In the novel *The Good Mother,* by Sue Miller, Anna is divorced from her husband and lives with her daughter, Molly. Her lover, Leo, moves in with her and the three develop what seems to be a comfortable family relationship. Anna and Leo feel relaxed and uninhibited around Molly and consider nudity nothing to be ashamed of. One night, when Leo is taking care of Molly, he takes a shower as she sits in the bathroom talking with him. When he steps out of the shower, she notices his genitals and asks if she can touch him. When he allows it, he is made uncomfortable by the sensation of having an erection. As a result of this incident, Anna loses custody of her daughter.

The particulars of the scene are not as important as the questions it raises. What is considered sexual abuse? Is a naked man "exposing himself" to a young child, or is he just performing his morning toilet? When an adult male wrestles or tickles a child and in playing touches the child's genitals, is this a form of harassment or abuse? If a biological father does these things is there any question of abuse? What about a stepfather?

These kinds of questions, both moral and legal, have yet to be answered, but there is clearly a growing concern about family sexual abuse in our society. This concern manifests itself in attitudes that are more conservative than they were a decade ago. A stepparent who believes in nudity and freedom of sexual expression, the "laid-back" attitude quite common in the sixties and seventies, might risk a family-court battle over child custody today.

The best intentions of a stepparent can sometimes be misinterpreted. Within the stepfamily home, it can be a very thin line that differentiates between acceptable expressions of affection and actions with sexual overtones, particularly between stepfathers and stepdaughters. Stepmothers, many of whom have daughters from previous marriages, need both to understand the fragility of their husband's position and at the same time to be aware that sexual interaction in stepfamilies can happen. Although much-needed attention is presently being give to sexual abuse, there is also the danger of making children more fearful and suspicious than necessary. Children who accuse a parent of abuse need to be heard, but care must also be taken to hear them correctly. They may be telling the absolute truth, expressing anger, acting out a fantasy, or showing a need for attention. As the biological mother, a woman must pay close attention to her children, particularly if they have suffered the trauma of divorce. Since the issues are always complex and few family members are able to remain objective, outside help is almost always called for if a child indicates that there have been sexual overtures. A therapist has the objectivity, training, and knowledge to help a child express real fears and realities and can recognize the signs of sexual abuse.

In the stepfamily with teenage children, sexuality is even more complicated because it is often combined with teenage anger and rebellion. According to Dr. Sonya Rhodes, in her book *Surviving Family Life,*

> Anger is a natural part of growing up, employed by teenagers like a weapon to blast themselves loose from the family.... [They must] break away from parents they love and stand, shakily, on their own. Anger helps the separation process. It's easier to leave people you love when you're angry with them. The child puts his anger between himself and his parents and creates distance, so he can begin to rely

> on himself. . . . The impact of adolescence shakes fam-
> ily life to its foundation.[2]

A stepfamily with teenagers is often in the process of trying to build a foundation for the new family, and the impact of adolescent children can be especially destructive. A heightened sense of sexuality in the home coupled with normal adolescent anger and rebellion is a heavy load for the family to carry. Even in biologically related families, there is a different atmosphere in a home with teenage children than in a home with toddlers. With teenagers around, there is an obsessive sense of the physical body. Teenagers are constantly occupied with how they look, and their bodies become important to their sense of self-worth.

At the same time, teenagers are more conscious and observant of their parents' physical appearance and more curious about their parents' sexuality. They are pulled one way by their curiosity at what their parents are up to and pulled another way by a need to believe that their parents are somehow not affected by the same sexual urges and fantasies that they are experiencing.

In biological families, children tend to separate their sexual natures from those of their parents and to relegate their parents' to some mild sexual area that is nonspecific in nature. When it is not mother or father but stepmother or stepfather who is sleeping in their parents' bed, however, the situation changes. It is more difficult for a stepchild to separate from a parent's sexuality, particularly if the parent is recently remarried. The comment "you don't understand" expresses the need of the adolescent to believe that he or she is different from the parents and is therefore allowed to make decisions in opposition to them. Having a parent who is obviously active sexually makes this separation more difficult.

To make the whole situation even more confusing, adolescents often feel a new power with their sexuality. It is a power they did not have as children and it is a power they are old enough now to use. They use it primarily with their peers. It is expressed in the clothes they wear, the language they use, and the innuendos they put into their conversations. Their clothes, their language, and the poses they strike are all ways of communicating among teenagers and since they more or less speak the same language and are all going through similar experiences, their sexual energy is channeled in relatively appropriate directions. When it is expressed in a stepfamily, however, it is not only misplaced but can be destructive. Stepchildren can act in a very seductive way toward their stepparents, sometimes unconsciously and sometimes with "malice aforethought." Rarely, however, do they really want sexual contact. They may like the idea of sexually attracting a stepparent, but more often this is another form of teenage rebellion. What better way to get at your parent than to flirt with the parent's spouse? What better way to assert one's power than to cause discomfort or desire in an adult? It is an effective way to play one parent against the other, an instinctive ability of many teenagers. It is important to realize that most teenagers do this without realizing it. It can be one of the "weapons" they use to separate.

Stepparents caught in this triangular situation find themselves with few options. The term used by therapists, "triangulation," becomes more like "strangulation" for the parents involved. One stepfather, James, remembers the years of his stepdaughter's adolescence. He tells how he walked "a wide circle" around her, careful never to be alone with her or give her any opportunity to accuse him of misconduct. He simply didn't trust her. She was angry at her mother and he was a prime target for that anger. In addition, James was convinced that his stepdaughter was sexually promiscuous and he felt that her activities reflected negatively on him. He did feel responsible for her, since her biological father lived in a distant city and assumed little responsibility for her. Although James gave her financial support and tried to advise her as a father figure, she refused to recognize his authority. "I had the responsibility but no authority," he remarked. The home environment was one of intense stress.

James's lowest moment came when he walked outside one night where his stepdaughter was in a parked car in front of the house with a boyfriend. When he couldn't even see their heads above the seat, he became so angry he threw a stone at the windshield and broke it. He describes those years as the "most exhausting, frustrating years of my life."

Many psychologists would argue that this man probably did feel a sexual attraction to his stepdaughter. She looked very much like her mother, but twenty years younger. It may sound like heaven to have a younger version of your beloved close by, but it can be hell. Living in such close contact with someone of the opposite sex who is not biologically related and therefore not automatically included in the strong incest taboo is tricky at best.

Combined with the feelings of sexual attraction is the frustration of having no real authority. Many stepfathers feel parental authority is denied them by their stepchildren, spouse, or both. According to Jean Giles-Sims and David Finkelhor in their study on child abuse in stepfamilies, "The blocking of authority may be particularly frustrating for stepfathers because of the expectation that fathers should be the head of household. . . . when a stepparent wants authority but does not have the resources to earn it, he or she may resort to the use of violence to gain control."[3]

Giles-Sims and Finkelhor also maintain that stress is an important factor in understanding violence in stepfamilies.

> Higher rates of both physical and sexual abuse among stepfamilies could be related to the unique stresses present in those families. Remarried families containing children from prior marriages must solve problems unfamiliar to other types of families. There are few institutionalized guidelines for solving the unique problems of this family structure including appropriate kinship terms, authority to discipline stepchildren, and family loyalty. Stepparents also experience contradictory pressures to assume some aspects of the parental role and to refrain from others. Without established guidelines, there are more opportunities for disagreements and stress associated with conflicting values and beliefs.[4]

Stress, lack of authority, absence of traditional guidelines, and sexual pressures all contribute to the difficulties of stepfathers and stepdaughters during the adolescent years.

In addition, not having the early years of shared affection and nurturing affects the relationship between stepparent and child. Without these early years of bonding, it is difficult to establish a workable father-daughter relationship. One father whose daughter came to live with him after thirteen years of separation found that he could not become an instant father.

Ron and his wife were divorced when their daughter was only two. He moved to a distant city and saw his daughter rarely. When she was fifteen, she asked if she could come and live with him and his new wife. Ron agreed because he was anxious to develop a relationship with this daughter he hardly knew. She was a beautiful girl who immediately made friends in school and became involved in many activities. Ron had never lived with a teenager and was uncomfortable with her late hours, long telephone calls, and increasing involvement with her new boyfriend. He considered himself a free spirit, and believed in freedom of expression and experimentation in relationships. But with his own daughter he felt different. He wanted her to conform to "safe" social norms. He found himself making stringent rules for her, about her clothes, telephone calls, dates, language—almost every aspect of her life. There was constant conflict over the rules, and even Ron was not comfortable with them.

Instead of having a beautiful reunion with his daughter, they did nothing but fight. Most troubling was that Ron recognized that he was sexually attracted to her. This attraction was so disturbing to him that he made rules and created conflicts to divert the attraction into constant conflicts. His daughter contributed to the antagonism as well, out of her own conflicted feelings for her father. Wanting to love his daughter, hoping to begin the father-daughter relationship they had never had, Ron found himself instead driven into torrents of rage and frustration. His daughter left after a few months and it has taken years for them to find a way to be together.

Ron is one of the few men who can admit to sexual attraction within the family. These feelings are more than denied, they are inadmissible—to a man, to his wife, and often to his daughter or stepdaughter. And yet the very intimacy of family life is conducive to physical attraction, and a man living with a female who has no biological ties to him cannot be expected to be oblivious to her.

In stepfamilies, tensions between stepfathers and stepdaughters can even force a woman to choose between spouse and child. When Ann and Dave married, her young daughter, Sarah, formed an affectionate relationship with Dave. When Sarah became adolescent, however, everything changed. Sarah developed into a beautiful girl and spent hours lying in the sun to get a tan, needed an extra hour in the bathroom every morning to wash her hair, and sat around the house in her nightgown painting her toenails or plucking her eyebrows— typical behavior for a teenager, but behavior that put a strain on her relationship with her stepfather. He was not comfortable with her household activities and began to make new rules. He insisted that her clothes be modest, set time-limits on the bathroom, and was critical of the time she spent "lying around." He scrutinized her friends and was reluctant to let her date.

Although Dave insisted that the rules were for her own good, Sarah chafed under what she perceived as a harsh regime. Even though Ann was not always comfortable with Dave's rules, she felt Sarah should obey her stepfather. Dave had taken on the primary financial responsibility for his stepdaughter and should therefore have some authority. As she got older Sarah became progressively more secretive about her activities, and a feeling of mistrust and suspicion began to grow in the family. When Sarah was caught breaking the rules, she became defiant. She became extremely critical of her stepfather's lifestyle—his clothes, his language, his tastes. Dave, who had just helped Sarah buy her own car, was understandably furious.

Ann was caught in the middle. Dave insisted, "It's your daughter or me!" and Sarah insisted, "You never stand up for me!" Ann could not convince Sarah to cooperate and she could not convince Dave to let up on the rules. After months of turmoil Dave insisted that Sara was ruining the marriage. Ann was torn. It seemed as though Dave and Sarah could not live in the same house. She loved Dave and did not want to leave him, but on the other hand she couldn't stop loving her child either.

One evening, after a quarrel with her parents, Sarah grabbed her car keys and started out of the house.

"It's too late for you to go out," Ann insisted. "I cannot allow you to leave."

Sarah ignored her mother and as she got into her car, Ann followed her out with an armload of the teenager's clothes.

"If you leave, take these with you," she shouted to her daughter, "and don't come back."

Sarah did not come back. She moved in with a friend until she finished high school and went away to college. Although Ann was the one who told her daughter to leave, it was clearly the result of the tension between Sarah and Dave. Without early physical bonding, without recognized parental authority, the heightened sense of sensuality in the home set up a dynamic that nobody was able to recognize or change. Ann was caught, and made the decision to break this destructive triangle in the only way she knew how.

When Dave said Sarah was ruining his marriage, he was not entirely wrong. His and Sarah's conflicted feelings created an untenable situation for his marriage. This family's ordeal is not uncommon in stepfamilies, and often it is the adolescent who separates. In Dave and Ann's family as in many other families that experience this severe disruption, the adolescent did eventually reunite with the parents. This usually takes years, however.

Again, a family therapist may be the only person with the objectivity to help family members through this most difficult period. It is important to remember, however, that this volatile situation in a stepfamily can be considered normal. Stress, confusions about authority, and normal adolescent anger and rebellion can all exist in stepfamilies. Family members find themselves caught in this combination of factors, and it is counterproductive to blame either parent or child.

Stepmothers can also have a difficult role as their stepsons develop sexually. The mother-son taboo is strong, although it does not have the same connotations of victimization as the father-daughter taboo. Nevertheless, legendary tales of mother-son incest involve brutal destruction and violence. Oedipus is not only destroyed but the children from his union with his mother meet violent deaths. In *The Holy Sinner*, a book by Thomas Mann based on the medieval legend of Pope Gregory, it is only through extreme penance—Gregory is shackled to a rock in the middle of a lake for seventeen years—and the exceeding mercy of God that Gregory is forgiven for unwittingly sleeping with his own mother.

Stepmother-stepson sexual liaisons are also treated as ultimately destructive. Phaedra kills herself after her stepson rejects her, and in Eugene O'Neill's *Desire Under the Elms* Abbie murders the baby born from her union with her stepson.

In the mother-son incest legends the "sin" is committed unwittingly, but nevertheless results in violence and destruction for all concerned. In the stepmother-stepson stories it is most often the stepmother who is destroyed. These stories imply that the mother-son taboo is so strong that it can only be broken under the most extreme circumstances, but the responsibility for maintaining the stepmother-stepson taboo rests with the female.

Although these dramatic examples are based on sexual roles more rigidly fixed than our society professes today, it is clear that stepmother-stepson sexual relationship not only undermines the very foundation of a family but is also destructive for the two individuals. A woman who expresses sexual attraction to her stepson is not only rejecting his father (whom he should respect), but also encouraging the son to violate his own integrity. Young men with strong sexual urges can easily lose sight of the repercussions of such a sexual liaison, but the stepmother cannot. To a great extent it is her responsibility to see that any sexual attraction or interaction is kept strictly under control. Although a young man can express "manly" desires, he should be considered the "child" within the family context, and the stepmother is the parenting adult.

Usually, however, such attractions are not clear-cut. A stepmother who wants to establish a bond with a stepson and wants to express genuine affection can find it hard to distinguish between familial affection and expressions that take on sexual overtones. In this context, therefore, it is usually better to err on the side of omission rather than of commission. If a stepmother feels concern and affection for her stepson she can usually find nonphysical ways to express them. Just as this can be tricky territory for a stepfather, a stepmother must be sensitive to the messages she is sending her stepson.

A friend tells of meeting his stepmother for the first time when he was eighteen. He had had little previous contact with his father and had traveled across the country to try and establish a relationship with him. His father had a new wife who was only a few years older than my friend. When he sensed that she was flirting with him, he was terrified. Although he hardly knew his father, the thought of getting involved with his father's wife was deeply disturbing. He left rather than let this happen and for years felt angry at his stepmother for her actions. It is possible that this stepmother only wanted to befriend him, and that because of her youth and attractiveness he felt threatened. Perhaps he felt attracted to her and resented her for these "bad" feelings in himself. This situation indicates, however, how important it is for a stepmother to be thoughtful about her responses to a stepson.

The makeup of a stepfamily also puts nonrelated children into close proximity. A romance between step-siblings is a slightly titillating subject; it has been the basis for a few teenage books and television programs. It can happen, although usually there is a natural inhibition between step siblings. A romance between step-siblings is more often the result of proximity than of true mutual affection. Parents may not be able to prevent such a relationship, particularly when the siblings are close in age, but these relationships almost always bring more pain than pleasure and should be discouraged.

When the siblings are of different ages, however, care must be taken to protect the younger child. Just as a child who is violated by someone he or she needs to trust, a child who is, or feels, sexually threatened in the home can suffer for many years afterward. In her diary, Virginia Woolf describes the painful experience of being sexually molested by her elder half brother when she was young. Although this cannot be the single cause of her mental illness and resulting suicide, the sense of hurt and violation she felt certainly affected her ability to relate sexually to men later in life. The experience of a child victimized by incest often results in deep emotional problems and forms of self-destruction. Although a stepmother cannot let suspicion undermine her relationship with the children in the stepfamily, a sense of openness and trust needs to be established so that a younger child feels able to talk about any actions that threaten or frighten him or her. The book *Treating the Remarried Family,* by Clifford J. Sager et al., maintains that the greatest trauma of household sexual abuse is the failure of the biological parent to protect. The child feels utterly abandoned, particularly in a stepfamily where the parent dismisses the child's complaint.[5]

All family members, both children and parents, need to feel safe in the home. A child can feel threatened by the sexual advances of siblings or parents, and a parent can feel threatened by the child as well. It takes a great deal of understanding and compassion by the adults in the family to avoid incidences of sexual trespassing or violence. As with so many other aspects of stepfamily life, these problems take on particular dimensions when the people involved are not biologically related.

To describe the many possible sexual infractions within the stepfamily can be discouraging. Living in close proximity, sharing personal space such as bathrooms and bedrooms, not having the taboos of a biological family, the stepfamily once again finds itself without guideposts or traditions to help.

Although many studies are being conducted on stepfamilies, there has not been time to do comprehensive longitudinal research—research over a period of years. Researchers, like stepfamily members themselves, don't yet know what will eventually work out as the best way to handle stepfamily problems. David Mills does suggest in his study, however, that trying to play a parenting role is often not successful for stepparents. He states, "Our clinical impression is that a significant number (but possibly less than half) of stepparents eventually adopt rules other than parental, and they and their families find satisfaction with this choice. It should be emphasized that a high proportion of those who do choose a parental role do *not* find it satisfactory."[6] Although Mills does not specify, it would seem that for a stepparent to play a parental role with adolescents, even if such a role was relatively successful before puberty, may not work. When sexual tensions are possible and the family feels acute stress, it may signal the time for the biological parent to take over the major role of parenting.

After talking to numerous families and family therapists, I think there seems to be agreement that the stepfamily needs clear boundaries and rules. It may be too much to ask nonrelated people living in close proximity to get along without these things. Barriers can help people come through difficult situations and keep people from acting out sexual feelings—i.e., help them keep thoughts separate from actions.

Privacy of the individuals needs to be respected, and nudity or sexually provocative clothing discouraged. Physical boundaries between family members (bedrooms, bathrooms) need to be clearly drawn. Careful consideration needs to be given to the circumstances when family members who are not biologically related are left alone together for long periods of time. The rules can be established by the consensus of family members, but lacking that ideal, the parents must have the final say and be in agreement.

These rules are best when they draw clear generational boundaries. The family needs to remember who is the child and who is the adult. What is acceptable for the adult sexually is not acceptable for the child. The only acceptable sexual interaction within a stepfamily is between the parents. In fact, the health of the stepfamily is dependent on the sexual well-being of the married couple. It is important to pay attention to and nurture that relationship while other family members are struggling toward independence. A healthy sense of sexual well-being in the parents will lessen sexual tensions in the family.

The success of the parents' relationship is often dependent on two things most families have little of—privacy and time. It often takes innovative planning and original thinking to find the time and privacy for physical love, but if the parents can convince themselves that what is good for their relationship is also good for the family, ways can be found to be alone together. Sexual relationships, when wrong, are horrible. But when a sexual relationship between two people is good, it is a source of strength and comfort for both. Stepparents need strength and comfort and they need each other. A stepfamily is only as strong as the people who have come together to form it, and together the parents can see the family through the most difficult times.

11

Birth and Death

BLEST BE THE TIES THAT BIND

TODAY, MORE THAN AT ANY OTHER TIME IN HISTORY, CHILDREN ARE BORN out of choice, not chance. In the past there were many forces at work in society to encourage childbearing. Religious instructions to "be fruitful and multiply" were widely accepted. Women were expected to be mothers; it was considered their most important function. Children were even useful; they were needed to work on the family farm or in the family business, and they were expected to care for parents who had reached old age. Since birth control was often inefficient or unavailable, large families were considered a fact of life.

Today, these factors are hardly applicable. With more options for women professionally, there are more possibilities for fulfillment other than having children. Rarely are children needed to work on the farm or in the family business and there is no guarantee that they will care for old and infirm parents. Children are also very expensive. Safe, reliable birth control is available. In a world already burdened with overpopulation

149

and shadowed by possible nuclear extinction, it is hard to make an argument for more children.

Nevertheless, although an increasing number of couples are choosing not to have children, most people want to have a child—their *own* child if possible. This desire to have a child crosses over all socioeconomic and educational borders. Although biological drives must play a role in this phenomenon, the urge for simple continuation of the species cannot be the only answer.

From classic paintings of the Madonna and Child to modern television advertisements, the image of a baby can be counted on to arouse positive emotions. It has been said that there is nothing more sentimental than a baby's shoe, and who can help but be won over by a baby's smile of recognition or the feel of a baby's hand clutched around a finger. To outsiders a new baby may look fat or cross-eyed, but to the family their baby is beautiful.

Even more important for parents, a baby absolutely *belongs* to them. There is satisfaction in that. A baby also represents new beginnings, new possibilities—a real and tangible purpose in life. During a television program on single mothers in Newark, New Jersey, a young unmarried father was interviewed. He was unemployed, had been in trouble with the law, and contributed little or no support for his son. When asked about his child, however, he answered, "Oh, my son's going to be fine . . . not like me. He'll get an education, I'll see to that. He'll be a lawyer or something." Although the young father had no realistic plan for accomplishing this dream, the look of hopeful optimism on his face when he spoke of his son was touching. His son was a new beginning in which anything was possible.

Of course babies grow up, and a teenager's dirty sneakers do not hold the same sentiment as baby booties, but few parents seem to regret having had children. In spite of the obvious problems in childbearing and child-rearing, having a child brings a dimension to life that most people feel is enriching. Children make you go beyond yourself; they enlarge your world and, as the years pass, "temper" your personality. They can make you proud and make you humble. They can prove the greatest joy and the greatest sorrow. And they do all this simply by being your children.

Lee and I wanted to have a child together from the beginning. If we had not had this desire, it would not have been so crucial for us to marry; we could simply have lived together. Getting together was not easy, however, and it took us five years from the time we fell in love until we were finally able to marry. Love wasn't the problem, but everything else was. Many times during those difficult years we despaired because there seemed to be so many obstacles. Many people needed to be considered and nobody seemed to be on our side, sometimes including ourselves. You cannot leave one relationship and enter another without a period of self-examination and without some effort to understand what was wrong and what was right in the first relationship. We had to pull away from each other, sometimes for long periods of time, before we could honestly come together again. Even after we were able to make a free and clear decision to live together, Lee was unable to obtain a divorce. But when we were finally together legally, and could legitimately have a child, it signified the permanence of our union.

Lee and I had no second thoughts about having a baby, although many stepparents have valid reservations. Many things need to be considered: the existing children, the willingness of both parents-to-be, and such practical considerations as where the baby will sleep and how much it will cost.

There is the possibility that a new child will cause the older children to feel displaced. A new baby in a stepfamily means that the "baby" of the family is no longer the baby, and the oldest child is also no longer the "oldest"—the new baby is for the moment the youngest of the whole family, and will be the oldest of any later children from the new marriage. The new baby starts its life in a "better" position than any of the other children since it is growing up in an intact family, whereas the other children are struggling with the conflicts and division of loyalties between two sets of parents. Also, watching a father rejoice over the birth of a new baby can be painful for the child who no longer lives in the father's home.

People pause at the expense of a new child, both financially and in terms of time. Men often feel reluctant to have more after remarriage because more children invariably involve more expenses and confusion. A baby requires space, money, and time that may need to be directed to existing children.

In spite of all the reasons *not* to have another baby, however, many parents, particularly women, want their own child. A woman who marries a man with children and who has never had any of her own is the person most "at risk" in a stepfamily. Being in a parental position but never being the real parent seems to be harder on women than it is on men. The stepmother is left feeling as though her nose is pressed against the window while the real party goes on inside without her.

Usually the decision to have a child in a new marriage turns out to be a good one, and statistically, stepfamilies that have new children adjust better than stepfamilies that don't. Babies can be an extremely unifying experience for the family. In our family this was certainly true. Although my stepchildren greeted the news of my pregnancy with caution, they greeted Adam's birth with unqualified enthusiasm. They adored him. They fought to hold him, hung over his bassinet, cooed and made faces at him; they were completely un-self-conscious about being silly with him. Photographs from that year show all the children gathered around with Adam in the middle grinning and kicking his heels up into the air to show off. All of the children spent more time with me because that was where the baby was, and we all felt closer.

After Adam's birth, Lee's children were no longer just my stepchildren, they were Adam's half brothers and half sister. Suddenly they had a real place in my life. I also had a place in their life that was not dependent on my marriage to their father. "Step" is a relationship that lasts only as long as the marriage lasts, but "brother" lasts forever. I would be their brother's mother as long as we lived.

It was this strong sense of bonding and love between the

siblings that brought me the most satisfaction. It was nice to feel that Adam would always have these people who cared for him and would look out for him in the future. It gave the term "extended family" a new meaning.

Although birth cannot save a marriage, it can save a stepfamily in that it forms a common bond among stepfamily members. This is particularly true with the children in the family. A new baby belongs equally to everyone. Many stepmothers speak of the satisfaction they feel when their stepchildren form close bonds with their half siblings. One stepmother, who invited her teenage stepson to live in during the late period of her pregnancy and the first months of her baby son's life, feels that this suggestion was the most important thing she has done as a stepmother. Even though they were so crowded that her stepson had to sleep on the couch, making him an integral part of the family during this period has meant the two boys have formed a close relationship that has been a pleasure to the family for many years.

Another stepmother says that the birth of her daughter changed the way she felt toward her two stepchildren. They are now her daughter's brother and sister; they are her daughter's family. This fact gives more substance and purpose to the stepmother's efforts to include her stepchildren in her life.

Jane Goodall tells a touching story drawn from her years of research with apes. An old female ape died and left a youngster who was still dependent. Of all the apes in the community, one came forward to care for the young one—his older brother. Evidently, the older ape brother, who was the equivalent in age to a teenager, played both a protective and nurturing role regarding his baby brother.

Although sibling rivalry has been observed since Cain and Abel, there is a bonding between siblings that is different from any other. It is the one biological bond that crosses over the boundaries between other family members in a stepfamily. This biological tie can help unify the family. In a stepfamily, where there are unavoidable conflicts and confused emotions, the relationship between half siblings tends to be satisfying for everyone.

A birth in the family can also make parents reexamine their marriage and reevaluate their life together. As Natalie described in chapter 6, having her own child enabled her to understand the feelings of her husband toward his two children.

Another woman who married a man with two sons tells how the experience of her daughter's birth marked the end of a "practice marriage" and the beginning of a real one.

Elizabeth was only twenty-two when she met Tony, whose wife had left him with two young boys. When they married four years later she would often say that she had married three people. She jumped into the role of "mega-mom," as she termed it, with gusto. She was sensitive to the trauma the boys had experienced at the loss of their mother and she wanted to make it up to them. Like many stepmothers, it was important for her to feel that she could do it all. She worked full-time, baked bread, cooked casseroles on Saturday, planned family trips, helped with homework, and was available to the boys when they needed to talk. She was the chief counselor, organizer, and structure-giver for her "three men." They appreciated it and often told her so. She was given credit for her efforts by everyone from family friends to her mother-in-law, and was considered a very successful stepmother by all who knew her.

When the older brother, Brian, left for college, the younger brother, Nat, joined a religious group which encouraged "psychic transferral." He spent hours sitting in the lotus position with a coconut placed before him. He explained that he was trying to put all his negative psychic energies into this coconut, which would be taken to a precipice on New Year's Eve and tossed over.

Since Nat had always been dramatic, Elizabeth didn't pay too much attention to his actions. She assumed he was adjusting to his brother's leaving for college, and decided to give him lots of room to work things out for himself. But it wasn't so easy. Nat then announced that he was a strict vegetarian and presented Elizabeth with lists of special grains, sprouts, and cheeses so that he could cook his own meals. The mess he left in the kitchen was a constant source of friction. Then he insisted on wearing pajamas to school. It seemed to Elizabeth that if she allowed one thing, Nat wanted more and more. She caught him "doing" hallucinogenic mushrooms in his room and found evidence of more drugs. Since Elizabeth had been so willing to take on the discipline, advice-giving, and structuring of the family, Tony was not prepared to step in at this point and make demands on his son.

As a Christmas present for the family, Elizabeth organized and paid for a ski trip during vacation. Shortly after they returned, Nat was in the kitchen making his usual mess as he put together his meal. When he walked out of the kitchen, leaving dirty pots and bits of vegetable peelings on the counter and open boxes on the table, Elizabeth blew up.

"What do I have to do—*pay* you to help me around here? Am I no more than your housemaid? I feel used . . . and I'm sick of it!"

Nat looked at Elizabeth as if he didn't understand what she was talking about. Elizabeth was so angry she started to cry. Brian, who was in the next room, heard her and came into the kitchen. He put his arms around Elizabeth.

"Thanks a lot for the vacation," he said to her. "We do appreciate what you do for us. Come on Nat, don't be such a slob. Give Elizabeth a hug."

Nat shuffled over and put his arms around his brother and Elizabeth. The three of them stood there together for a moment.

"This is the way we used to hug Mom when we were little," Nat said softly.

Elizabeth knew that Nat was trying to say "thank you" to her but she could also hear the yearning for the mom who had left—the mom who was not there buying bean sprouts, helping with homework, or organizing ski vacations. Even though she was absent, she was still his mom. No matter what Elizabeth did, she was not Nat's mother.

Elizabeth realized that she wanted her own baby, and when she became pregnant she felt the need to get things' straightened out with Nat before her baby was born. She made an appointment for him to see a therapist and he agreed to go, although reluctantly. After meeting with Nat, the therapist asked to meet with Elizabeth and Tony.

"I don't need to see Nat again," she said. "He'll be fine. You two have the problem. You have not really gotten together on what you want from each other or your children. You've given Nat too much power and he's calling the shots. You two have to concentrate more on each other and less on Nat. Just agree to the rules and he'll come around."

At first this made no sense to Elizabeth but she tried to make some rules. Nat was not to wear pajamas to school, he was not to do drugs, and he was to spend more time on his homework and less time with the coconut. Nat essentially ignored her. Tony, who was in the process of changing jobs, was away often and when he was home he avoided conflict with Nat. Elizabeth railed and ranted for months, crying and storming around the house in anger. When she suggested that they go back to the therapist, it was Nat who said, "Don't worry, Elizabeth, I think we can handle this ourselves."

It's true, she thought. Nat *is* in control.

When her daughter was born, shortly afterward, Elizabeth's thinking began to shift. She stopped thinking about Nat so much and began to think about the father of her child. Who was this man she had been married to for almost ten years? What did she want from *him?* She had been so busy role-playing, being "mega-mom" to *his* kids, that she had not really paid much attention to their relationship. Every day had been built around Nat and Brian—their lives, their problems, their futures. It was as though she and Tony had never gotten around to learning much about each other. She began to think that their marriage had gotten lost in family life.

She realized that she had perceived the success of her marriage in terms of her role as mega-mom, filling the role left by the mother who was not there. But she began to see that she was playing a role, and no matter how well she played it there was still something missing. They were not her sons and she was not their mother. Being with her baby made her realize that the particular bonding of mother and child would inevitably be missing between stepmother and stepchild. She had been working to earn the love of her stepsons, but although they cared for Elizabeth, they could not satisfy her craving for motherhood. In some ways, she saw, she was asking them for something that they couldn't give her.

She realized she didn't want to be mega-mom anymore. She wanted to be with her daughter and Tony. With her own child, she didn't need to play a role. She was "legitimate." Elizabeth quit work and resolved to step back from Nat's dramatic efforts for attention. She became more confident in knowing how she felt about the boys rather than needing "credit" or appreciation from them.

Most important, the birth of their child forced Elizabeth and Tony to turn toward each other rather than running parallel races. Elizabeth has had a second child, and now she feels that she can look back on a "practice marriage that failed." Now she and Tony are building a real and new marriage.

Elizabeth is not sure her marriage would have survived without the birth of her daughter. Having her own child enabled her to distance herself from her stepsons in a healthy way by giving her a sense of legitimacy. She no longer needed to prove anything by playing a role, and she no longer ached for a kind of response that her stepsons were unable to give. At the same time, she felt a greater commitment to her marriage, and was able to take a hard look at her relationship with Tony.

A birth in a stepfamily often has this positive effect. It helps put the stepmother-stepchild relationship on a more realistic plane, enriches the love relationship between the parents, and gives the family a unifying "blood tie."

Lee and I had two children, Adam and Miranda. Their births, however, enclosed the tragedy of death. The presence of Adam and the arrival of Miranda helped us all survive the pain of my son Nicholas's drowning. Although the loss of a child is unusual, our experience can illuminate the process of grieving that many families experience.

A year after Adam was born we bought a house in Connecticut. We wanted a place to go on weekends with the children and had found a wonderful old clapboard house with swimming rights on a nearby millpond. We spent a weekend moving in furniture and on the following weekend we were joined by Lee's brother and his family, which meant there were ten children in all.

We were cooking hamburgers while the children swam in the pond. Nicky had recently started swimming with a snorkel mask and would spend endless amounts of time floating around on the surface of the water looking down into its murky depths.

Suddenly Lee noticed Nicky was missing. Within minutes Lee and his brother were diving and searching in the water for him. Seven other children were close by when he disappeared but no one could figure out where he had gone. We called and searched, hoping he had gone into the woods and not down into the muddy water. I had been raised at a seashore that sloped easily and predictably toward the deep, and it had never occurred to me that a country pond could have depths so dark and tangled that visibility was virtually nonexistent. We called the police and when they arrived they brought skin divers who dived repeatedly in wet suits into the pond. Still they found nothing. As the agonizing afternoon wore on, the police managed to pull out the stopper from the dam and drain the pond. When the water was finally gone, Nicholas lay at the bottom.

There is no greater blow than the loss of a child; everything is changed forever. Statistically, 90 percent of parents divorce after the death of a child. This stunning statistic is the result of pain, grief, depression, and the unfortunately human compulsion to blame someone. Couples often end up blaming themselves or one another. If they retreat into private grief, or cope with their pain by finding comfort elsewhere, the family dissolves. Certainly I experienced feelings of emptiness and despair, but because Lee was not Nicky's father he was able to help me through them. Lee ministered to me, not leaving my side for over two months. I also had Adam, who demanded attention every day. He was bubbling and happy and got me up every morning with infectious cheerfulness. Pete, Willy, and Kate seemed to draw closer to me. Just as Adam's birth had provided a bridge between us, so did Nicky's death. I became pregnant again and had our daughter Miranda the following spring. For me, giving life helped to lighten the weight of death.

My daughter Kristin, however, did not get the same comfort from this other family. Lee's children were saddened at Nicholas's death, but Kristin was devastated. Nicky had been Kristin's closest ally during the years of my divorce and remarriage. During this period my life was in turmoil, and I was not the calm, attentive mother I would have liked to have been. Working, taking care of the children, and sorting out my relationship with Lee preoccupied me so much that Nicky and Kristin grew to depend on each other.

When Lee and I did marry, they had a new place to live in a new city, new brothers and sister, and a new father to adjust to. They were able to deal with the changes around them because they had each other. They were partners. At home, they helped each other sneak unwanted food away from the table in their napkins. They took up for one another before their step-siblings or Lee. They took the long airplane trips together to see their father in California. Most important, they created a fantasy world in which they were safely together, a world of superheroes and derring-do that they whispered about in their own special language. In this world they were safe from uncertainty. They had created it and had control of it. Together they could do anything.

And then Nicky drowned. Kristin saw her older brother, whom she saw as the bravest and strongest person in her young life, taken from her in a senseless accident. He was her best friend, her "anchor to windward," and then he was gone. There was no way she could make sense of this. There was no sense, no justice or fairness.

What happened to Kristin was the fulfillment of the deepest fears of childhood: she had been abandoned, first by Nicky and then, in part, by me and her father. She saw her mother being pulled away from her, busy and sometimes overwhelmed with the new family, and her father living three thousand miles away.

For Kristin, Nicky's death caused a great fearfulness. For

years she was afraid of dying, and wanted no pets or anything that she might lose. She withdrew to the safety of her third-floor room, alone and separate from the noise and closeness of family life. I saw that she was retreating to her room, spending more and more time reading, but I learned only later that she retreated in part because she didn't want to "burden" me with her fears and anxieties. She went away to boarding school when she was sixteen and then to college. Fate still had one more blow in store for her. When she was a college sophomore, her father died of cancer. Although separated by thousands of miles, Kristin and her father had developed a close relationship, and for him also to be cut down in the prime of his life left her bereft. After the funeral she took nothing from his home except a jacket from the set of *Kojak,* the television series he had written for. I think she wanted something of his to wrap around her.

Watching a child suffer is very hard for a mother. I saw that Kristin was bewildered and in pain and yet it was difficult for me to help her. My life was different from hers; I had new babies, a husband, and three stepchildren while her life was empty of all family except for me.

When there is a tragedy in a stepfamily, everyone grieves differently, depending on the extent to which the tragedy affects them. Lee's children's loss in Nicholas's death could not be compared to Kristin's, and they had never known her father so were incapable of sharing her grief at his death in a meaningful way. Sometimes members of a stepfamily grieve alone.

Despite the difficulties in her life, Kristin is a survivor. Over the years she has worked through her fears and grown to understand better how she wants to live her life. She has remained somewhat aloof from the family but keeps in touch with us. She has begun to move away from her fears by obtaining her driver's license, getting a puppy, and investing in a house. She loves gardening and admits that this is partially because a garden is an environment she can control. Her interest in flowers has provided a way for her and Lee to build a relationship that was too difficult for them a few years ago, and she has redesigned our garden with him. Now she feels free to talk about her brother and father, and we discuss the years before and after their deaths frequently. Kristin's and my relationship as mother and daughter has been greatly affected by my being a stepmother, but rather than this being a negative for us, we have continued to work together toward mutual respect and love.

Kristin's and my experience is uncommon, but there are certain truths about the deaths we experienced that are applicable to most stepfamilies. Children who fear loss after the dissolution of their original family have reason for their fear. The end of their original family means that a unit will no longer exist for solace and comfort. If a member of their biological family dies, their stepparent or step-siblings will not feel the same way that they do. Having a parent become a stepparent shifts their allegiance from the original family to the stepfamily and this too can be threatening. Although their family may have expanded as a stepfamily, children often feel more alone without the security of their original family unit. Stepparents need to be sensitive to these fears in their children.

A woman who marries a widower has a special role as a stepmother. For a child, a mother's death is one of the most traumatic things that can happen. Recovering from this loss can take a long time, and expressions of grief can take forms that are not easily recognizable. Nevertheless, grieving must progress. Even though the loss of a parent or spouse is tragic, this loss cannot be the primary focus of a family indefinitely.

Studies have shown that a person moves from shock and sadness on through anger toward final acceptance and resolution after a loved one's death. If, however, a person becomes "stuck" during this process and remains either angry or immersed in grief, often an outside force is needed to help him or her move onward. Sometimes it is the stepmother who is this outside force. A stepmother represents the future for a family who has lost a mother, not the past.

Because a family is a changing system, a mother's death inevitably comes at a time when her relationship with her children is in the process of evolving. If she dies when the children are quite young, she will probably be remembered in an idealized or romantic way. If she dies, however, when her children are pubescent or adolescent, many conflicts, anxieties, and other such feelings that are normal between adolescents and parents may never be resolved. The child is left with no ability to continue the normal process of separating and finally establishing a mature relationship with his or her mother.

One stepmother who married a widower with a teenage daughter finally realized that her stepdaughter was not only suffering from shock and loss from her mother's death but also carried with her the burden of unresolved feelings.

Susan, who had been through a traumatic divorce and lived alone with her two children, a son and daughter, met Charles a year after his wife, Helen, was killed in an accident. Their attraction was that of opposites. Susan was by nature a gregarious, talkative person. She loved bright colors, enjoyed staying busy all the time, and looked at life in a positive, upbeat way. Charles and his daughter, Kate, on the other hand, were reserved and found it difficult to express their feelings. Although Susan was open to anything they wanted to tell her about Helen, there was a blanket of silence about their life before her. Their reserve indicated to Susan that they were still grieving, and she resolved to help them by encouraging them to express their grief openly. She was not going to try to replace Helen or compete with her, but she was anxious to comfort and help both Charles and Kate.

When Charles and Susan married, she and her two children moved into Charles's house, which had three bedrooms. This meant, however, that Susan's daughter and Kate had to room together until an addition could be built onto the house. This arrangement caused immediate friction between them. Susan promised the two girls that the situation was temporary and things would be better as soon as the house was enlarged, but Kate seemed to resent even the idea of change. Kate perceived Susan's plans for remodeling the house as having her home taken away. It was frustrating for Susan to be perceived as ruining Kate's home, but it was also clear that the combined families needed a different kind of space. Kate's unhappiness pervaded the new family. Nothing seemed to please her. She was unhappy at home and unhappy at summer camp. She disliked the public school she attended but did not want to change to private school.

Susan's attempt to encourage Kate to talk about her problems met with gloomy silence. Susan began to feel that her energy was being sapped by this unhappy child. Worst of all, her own two children were being pulled into the gloom. They had not asked to be a part of this family but nevertheless were experiencing the sense of unhappiness that overshadowed the household.

Susan finally decided she had to learn more about Helen. She felt like a private investigator—trying to ask carefully worded questions, talking to neighbors and other people in the community. Slowly she learned that Charles's previous marriage had been troubled and he had simply withdrawn, working ten to twelve hours a day at the office. Helen and Kate had been having their own difficulties, which were far from being resolved when Helen was killed. The combination of these unresolved family problems and Helen's death had basically paralyzed Charles and Kate by the time Susan met Charles. It occurred to her that her own brightness was probably one of the reasons Charles was attracted to her. It was her role to jolt the family out of a lethargy that had existed even before Helen's death. She realized that she was dealing not only with the family grief but with long-term family problems that had never been resolved. Circumstances from before she had met Charles were affecting not only her life but her children's lives as well. In her efforts to help her stepdaughter, she had shortchanged her own children.

Susan got mad. She was angry at her stepfamily and angry at herself for letting things get so bogged down. She was suddenly tired of always being understanding and cheerful. The situation had to change . . . someone had to rock the boat. Her anger led her to insist that although she understood Kate's grief there was nothing she could do about it. The time had come to move on and look toward life and the future, not linger in the past. She insisted that Kate's depression and grief were selfish and self-centered and affected the lives of people who could do nothing about it. She told her stepdaughter to stop feeling sorry for herself and to realize that there were other people in the world. Susan felt the need to defend her own children from the negative attitudes that pervaded the family.

Although Susan's anger caused great turmoil in the family initially, her demonstrativeness had a positive affect. By "acting out" for her stepfamily, she brought some of their anger and grief out in the open. The atmosphere in the family began to change and Susan could see a more positive attitude in Kate. As is often the case with stepmothers who become so frustrated that they stop trying to accomplish the impossible, Susan realized there was only so much she could do. She could be an example of a positive approach to life, she could pay more attention to her own children's adjustments and needs, and she could help her husband enjoy life again and participate more fully in their marriage. By concentrating on the positive things that she was able to do with her life, she set an example that was beneficial for the family as a whole.

This does not mean that Susan and her family are living happily ever after; the past cannot be revoked, and will continue to be a part of the family life. But by shifting her energy from trying to understand and heal the loss into working toward a new and positive family atmosphere, Susan finds she is better able to cope with the day-to-day problems.

The death of a father and husband also greatly affects the relationships within a stepfamily. Sometimes this marks a definite severance between stepmothers and stepchildren, but it can also result in a closer bond.

When Katherine married Winston, an artist, she knew she had committed herself to a sensitive man who struggled with deep emotional problems. His artistic personality was plagued by periods of severe depression.

Winston had shown her a picture of his ten-year-old son, Louis, the first time they met. Louis lived thousands of miles away with his mother, and because of the bitterness of the divorce and the distance, Winston had seen little of his son over the years. Katherine had no children of her own and she was struck by the depth of emotion Winston felt for his child, but she also saw how fearful Winston was about seeing him again. After they had been married a year, she and Winston made arrangements for Louis to fly to New York. As the arrival time approached they were both nervous and distracted. When this young boy got off the plane, however, he looked so childlike and frightened that Katherine resolved to do everything in her power to make his visit perfect. The visit went well, with Katherine working to provide a secure environment where father and son could build a relationship. Louis continued to visit his father and Katherine on a regular basis.

As Louis got older, however, he became resentful of Katherine's presence. He was artistic like his father, and admired him passionately. He wanted to spend every hour with him in the studio. Louis seemed to feel that Katherine was Winston's "caretaker," but was not as intellectual or artistically insightful as he, or as Louis himself. She remembers how, although they ate their meals at a round table, Louis always shifted his chair just enough that his back was slightly to her.

Nevertheless, Katherine knew how deeply Winston felt for his son, and she worked hard to create a sense of family when they were together. Hers was the stable personality and she was able to help Winston with both the struggles of being an artist and the bouts of depression that plagued him.

As Louis grew into manhood he became gloomy and depressed. Perhaps because he felt anger at being "abandoned" by his father as a child, Louis became more hostile toward Winston. When he visited, he would be secretive and unpredictable. He would disappear for hours and return home drunk. Winston was battling alcoholism and seeing his son embarking on the same path was particularly painful for him. Katherine continued to try to smooth things over, hoping the visit would somehow go all right.

When he graduated from high school, Louis came to live with Katherine and Winston. After only a few weeks, however, they realized it wouldn't work. Louis was moody and unpredictable and caused constant worry for his father. After he left, Louis and Winston maintained their relationship primarily through letters, and as Louis got older he withdrew. He rarely got in touch and there would be spans of time when no one knew exactly where he was. Winston became worried and frustrated with his son, expecting the worst.

When Winston became ill and was confined to a hospital, Louis did not write or come to see him. It became clear that he was dying. When Winston had only a few weeks to live, Katherine finally found Louis.

"You will have to live with yourself and this rejection of your father," she said angrily. "He will soon be gone and there will be no way to make it up to him."

Although Louis did come to see his father, he stayed only a few days and left without saying good-bye. By then Winston was so ill with cancer that he could hardly even recognize anyone, and perhaps it was too painful for his son to see him. When he died Louis returned for the funeral, but in such bad condition that Katherine literally had to find clothes for him to wear and had to help him through the service.

A few months later, when Katherine was going through some old books, she found a book of children's poetry that Winston had inscribed to Louis when he was a little boy. She sent it to Louis, but with a note that said that if he lost the book she "would put a curse on him."

Katherine could later see that she was reacting to the months of stress that she had experienced as Winston died, as well as to a deep sense of anger at Louis for the way he had treated both her and his father. She had watched Winston suffer so much and she felt that his son had exacerbated his pain.

Louis wrote Katherine a letter in which he said that she didn't need to put a curse on him—she had put a curse on him long ago.

Except for the angry phone call before Winston's death, this was the first time Katherine and Louis had openly expressed their anger and hostility toward one another. As she reread the letter over and over, Katherine began to realize that she did not really want to lose Louis. He was a part of Winston, one of the few things she had left. He was much like his father, both in his artistic talent and in his personality. Katherine wrote a letter of apology. Louis responded with his own apology and the two of them began a slow but steady friendship.

Katherine eventually saw that she and Louis had always felt in competition for Winston. Each had wanted Winston to love him or her the best, and each had felt the other stood in the way. Now that there was no Winston to compete for, they were able to be helpful to each other.

When Louis had his first art show, Katherine attended. In a short speech to the people gathered to see his work, he said, "I am happy to be here and I am particularly happy that my stepmother is here with me."

Louis and Katherine have continued to build their friendship. They can now talk about their past life and can share common interests. For Katherine, who has no children of her own and considered Winston the most important person in her life, her friendship with Louis has been a great source of comfort and satisfaction. But before they could get this far, they had to confront each other with their feelings of mistrust and anger.

In considering the many aspects of birth and death in stepfamilies it is clear that even these basic realities of life take on new and important dimensions when they occur in such families. Although parents and children rarely realize what is ahead of them when they come together to form a stepfamily, they are truly embarking on a journey filled with joys and pains that take on special meaning because of the family unit. In talking with stepmothers about how birth and death have affected their lives, it is rewarding to hear how birth can strengthen the family bonds, and it is encouraging to hear how the human spirit can triumph over the pain and adversity of death. Stepfamily members can find comfort and solace through one another "in sickness and in health . . . for better or for worse," and they do this by choice, not chance. It is in the choosing that their lives can be enriched and the meaning of family can be expanded.

12

Leaving the Nest

EVEN STEPMOTHERS GET THE BLUES

THE STRUCTURE OF FAMILIES IN AMERICA IS SHIFTING, NOT ONLY because of the rapid increase in stepfamilies but also through the extended number of years that children are financially dependent upon their parents. With educational expenses high and more students seeking graduate education, many children find themselves in need of parental assistance well into their twenties. Even after college, many students return home because separate housing is initially too expensive for them. Added to this is the phenomenon of taking time off from academia, a practice not only condoned but sometimes encouraged by academic institutions. Many young people simply take more time before they set up an independent existence for themselves.

This change, caused by a combination of both economics and attitudes, means that adolescence is extended. On the other end, childhood is shortened in our society by exposure to the media, and earlier awareness of adult and world problems, sexuality, and exposure to drugs and violence. As outlined in chapter 9, the period of adolescent growing up and breaking away can be extended from prepubescence until the mid or late twenties. That is a long time for everyone, the parent as well as the child.

Nevertheless, the goal for everyone during these years is independence for the adolescent. Although some biological parents, either subconsciously or actively, undermine their children's attempts at finding an independent life, few stepparents want a continued dependent relationship, either emotionally or financially, with their stepchildren. This can mean that a stepparent can play a positive role in helping stepchildren evolve independently.

Parents often have a strong protective urge toward their children. They know the world is a rough place out there, and they want to do what they can to alleviate the pain and struggle their children must go through in order to mature. They often have a high emotional investment in their children, which makes it difficult for them to distance themselves from their children's struggle. As one therapist put it, parents often take too much credit for their children's successes and too much blame for their failures. As their children mature and make the necessary steps to leave the nest, finding the right balance between healthy distance and necessary nurturing can be very difficult.

Sometimes a child must be given an extra push to get out of the nest, and this can be extremely difficult for a parent. Although helping a husband give his child that extra push toward independence can make the stepmother seem cold and distant, it can also be a positive aspect of stepmothering.

A man who grew up in Ireland once described the wind as being "as cold as a stepmother's heart." In spite of the obviously negative connotations of this phrase, there are times in a family when it is imperative that someone have the distance and ability to insist that children stand on their own. Two stepmothers who helped their husbands hold back financial support for their children during "break-away" periods can look back and know that their "coldness" was helpful.

Pat's stepson Paul was the youngest of five children in the

stepfamily. The older children had managed to get through college with a combination of grants, loans, summer work, and parental help. By the time Paul was in high school the burden of his parents' educational expenses had lessened, and since Paul was unhappy in public school, Pat and her husband Eric paid for him to attend boarding school for two years. Paul was something of a dreamer, and although he did fairly well in school he never found any special interest that he could pursue for any length of time. Particularly irritating to Pat was his disinterest in contributing financially toward his education. She felt that her own two children had not only worked hard to help pay for college but had also matured a great deal in the process. Paul, on the other hand, never even seemed to get around to finding a steady summer job, and could spend hours playing computer games or picking out chords on his electric guitar. After one semester of poor grades in college, Paul dropped out, saying he wanted time to think. His father said that if he wasn't going to be in school he would have to support himself. Paul agreed, and got a job and an apartment that he shared with friends.

Within a month Paul began to call and ask for money. He needed to install a phone, his car had broken down and he had to buy a new clutch, etc. Then he quit his job, saying that he wanted to concentrate on starting a band. At this point Pat stepped in. Either Paul was independent or he was not. If he wasn't, then he should be back in school or doing something constructive toward his education. If he was independent, then he had to *be* independent. Independence meant paying his own way. Eric agreed.

It wasn't so hard refusing to advance Paul money for his rent or a telephone bill, but when he called home for money because he had broken his glasses and needed to buy a new pair, Eric wavered. Pat was adamant, however.

"Buying your own glasses is part of being independent," she insisted. "As long as Paul has this net to catch him whenever he has trouble, he will not take responsibility for himself."

Refusing to send money for Paul's glasses did not suddenly

make him take total responsibility for himself, but he realized that he could not continue to call home for cash. He did use the stepfamily as a resource, however, and moved into his stepsister's apartment for a few months. She was able to insist that he get a part-time job, do his share of household work, and help pay the bills. She was more effective in this than either Pat or Eric had been and her involvement lessened the strain between them. As the "baby" in the family, Paul was used to being watched after, and it took continued pushing by family members to help him strike out on his own.

Elizabeth, who struggled for family control with her stepson Nat in the previous chapter, also found that she finally had to take a hard line. After one year in college Nat dropped out to travel in Europe for a year. Although it was agreed that he could do so, he had to pay his way. When Nat called his father for money from some small town in southern Italy, Elizabeth put her foot down.

"You can't do it," she insisted. "He wants to be independent and he has to learn that his decisions have consequences. He won't starve—Nat is much too clever for that."

Elizabeth was right. Nat managed to work his way through Europe and returned home after a year as pleased about his ability to support himself as about his travel adventures.

If Paul and Nat had made their requests for money to their biological parents, they probably would have received it. The need to protect one's biological child continues even after that child is grown. With the distance and conviction of a stepparent, however, these difficult decisions could be made. Both young men gained a greater sense of self-sufficiency through their experiences, although at the time they were angry at the "coldness" of their stepmother's heart.

Many stepfamilies have found it necessary to refuse to allow adult stepchildren to live in the home. Although a young child may have no alternatives, children over eighteen can usually make other arrangements if necessary. Although each family situation is different, and even adult children may have special needs that require time spent at home, a stepmother cannot accomplish the impossible. One stepmother's experience, although unusual because of her closeness in age to her stepchildren, is instructive in that she was able to recognize an impossible situation.

Pam was only one year older than her husband Robert's oldest son when she married. She didn't expect her husband's four children to like her—after all, she had "taken him away," and she had only graduated from their high school a couple of years before. She just hoped that they wouldn't be too mean to her.

She did have a fantasy, however, of their all being one big happy family . . . with her being one of the kids. She envisioned them all doing things together out-of-doors—hiking and camping and sitting around the camp fire singing songs. She soon found out that the happy family she had married was not happy at all. She said, "The kids all turned out to be brats! With big problems and terrible grammar."

It soon became clear to Pam that Robert's children recognized no boundaries. When they visited they simply took over. She was neither their "sister" nor their "mother," but she was able to keep her good humor during the relatively short visits. Although it seemed to her that chaos reigned, it was never for very long. She also hoped that she could in some way participate in their lives and even wanted to make up to them for the fact that their father was no longer living with them.

When the two younger sons asked to come and live with Pam and Robert, she agreed with some reluctance. She knew their father wanted them nearby and that they saw her relaxed way of life as an interesting contrast to their previous home life. Pam had a new baby, and she hoped that their joint interest in her new son would give their life a new structure. Trying to take care of the baby and keep some order in her life was almost impossible with the two teenage boys living there, however. Robert was traveling most of the time so she was left with his sons. One day when she had just put the baby to sleep, she walked into the kitchen to find the sink filled yet again with dirty pots and dishes. Furiously she put all the dirty dishes— with bits of food still on the plates and the liquids still sloshing around in the cups—in a large basin, then took that up to her stepsons' room and dumped them all on the bed. She made her point, but she also realized that she could not mother these young men. She was too young herself.

A few weeks later she returned home in the evening to find her stepsons having a party. Rooms were filled with teenagers who were clearly drinking and doing drugs. Robert was out of town, and as Pam held her baby in her arms and looked at the group of people gathered in her house, it was immediately clear that she had absolutely no control. Her demand that they get out was met with smiling invitations for her to join them. It occurred to her that she could call the police but she was reluctant to take such a drastic step. Feeling helpless, she left and spent the night at a nearby Ramada Inn . . . but from then on she knew that her stepsons had to go. Even though they had not yet finished high school and obviously needed adult supervision, she was not the one to do it.

"At first I couldn't believe I was making these ultimatums," Pam later said. "But admitting that I simply couldn't do it was such a relief. Then I realized that I didn't even *want* to take care of Robert's boys."

Although she knew that her husband felt guilty about leaving them, and she herself had initially even felt guilty about "taking" their father, feeling guilty did not make the family any more able to live together. Although she refused to let the boys live with her, Pam did make an effort to remain friendly and helpful to them. She refused to pretend to be something she could not be, but at the same time she tried to be constant in what she could be—a nonjudgmental friend, and someone they could talk to.

Pam's insistence that she could not live with her stepsons was brave in a way. She admitted that she could not play a mothering role, and it was probably better to have a relationship with her stepsons that she could maintain than trying to continue in a pattern that was destructive for all.

Helping push children out of the nest is only one part of the separation process, however. Some children need the push, but others need either a longer period of nourishment or a "place to come back to." More than one stepmother who has married a man with grown children has been surprised to find those children returning home to live with father. As one stepmother said, "I married Philip with the idea that we would have a glorious life together . . . just the two of us. I mean his children were all in college or out, for heaven's sake . . . and then they all came back!"

In our own family, Lee's two sons lived with us, each for approximately a year after they graduated from high school. Pete was working as a house painter, and since he had income he contributed toward household expenses. He seemed content to be with us but he never furnished his room in the personal ways that would have made it his own. It felt as though he never really moved in—we were just a temporary way station. When Willy lived with us he was in school, and was therefore not expected to help financially. By this time we had developed a friendly relationship, and I personally found their time with us rewarding. Especially satisfying was their relationship with Adam and Miranda. Living in the same household day after day enabled the siblings to become closer, and they were able to form a bond that had not been possible when Pete and Willy only visited. I also found that I grew to *like* them. They seemed much more approachable than in our earlier years together—I could be more of a friend than a parenting figure.

This does not mean that things always went smoothly. Adults living with a family do not conform to the same rules that apply for younger children. They invariably have a life of their own, and even such everyday occurrences as mealtimes cannot be rigidly enforced. I learned to try to keep a schedule for our younger family while realizing that it was unrealistic to expect Pete and Willy to be on time for meals, or to arrive home at a certain hour at night. Although it seemed at times more like having boarders than children, we were all able to get along well together. Actually, I believe they were more comfortable living with their stepmother during this period than they would have been living with their biological mother. I did not feel threatened by the way they lived their lives or made their decisions, and my distance gave them the space they needed at this time of their lives.

All families who have adult children living in the home find themselves making special adjustments. In this respect, stepfamilies are not that different from biological families. The phenomenon in America is relatively new, so many families are finding ways to accommodate young adults in the home. In the past, particularly in agrarian communities or in families where young adult children were expected to contribute to the family income, the roles of children and parents were fairly well defined. Today, however, adult children in the home usually consider their stay only a temporary stage in their lives. They are often saving money for their own place, taking time off from academia or working and saving money for further education. In this sense, although they can be expected to participate to some extent in family life, they do not actually feel that they have the same investment in the home that parents still do.

One mother planned for the possibility of her children returning home to live. In her mind, the children would all contribute to the cost of hiring a cleaning person once a week; each child would be in charge of at least one meal, and they would take turns doing the shopping and errands. When her two adult children did in fact return home to live, she found her well-thought-out plans remained just that—plans. The reality was something different. Since the children were both working and saving money for further education, asking them to contribute considerable sums to housecleaning or food simply meant they would be less able to pay tuition. Their idea of preparing a family meal was canned spaghetti and hamburgers or ordering in pizza. Their idea of a clean house fell far short of her ideas on the matter.

After some initial frustration and anger, this mother finally sat down and figured out what she actually liked to do in terms of housekeeping and what she really disliked. She enjoyed preparing meals and found satisfaction in general housecleaning. She hated cleaning up after dinner, doing laundry, running errands, and picking up or delivering at airports, trains, etc. She was able to work out a fairly workable schedule in which the jobs got done, with everyone doing things they didn't find objectionable. Although the children did not contribute toward rent or food, they were responsible for their own clothes, telephone bills, and automobile expenses.

Each family must make its own arrangements according to its needs and resources. A stepmother's role with adult children at home is not that different from a biological mother's. She needs to decide what she is happy doing for her family and what she feels is their responsibility, and must express her needs.

The key to her role with her stepchildren, however, is her husband's role in the household. As one stepmother put it, "I can demand and beg and try to coerce my children and stepchildren to help around the house, but it is the example of [my husband] Lawrence that makes the difference. He helps; he's a great cook, loves to bake bread and fancy desserts. He will vacuum a room if it needs it, and generally gives everyone the feeling that we are all in this together. *He* doesn't treat me like a housemaid, so the children don't either. And best of all, he doesn't make an issue of it . . . he just does it."

One special circumstance can exist in a stepfamily with adult children, however. Children who did not grow up in their father's home may come to live because they want to establish a closer bond with their father. Since they are usually coming to live during a time when they are also trying to break away and become independent, the push and pull of these conflicting needs can be difficult for everyone. A stepmother in this situation can only step back and try to give her husband and his child enough room to work out their relationship, keeping her eye on the fact that their stay will not last forever. If possible, she should not compete with the child for the father's love and attention. Her relationship with her husband is very different from that of his child and there should be plenty of room for both. As one stepmother observed, "Love is not like a bag of sugar: by using it you're not going to run out. There's always more love to give."

Many stepmothers have found that they were able to

establish a separate relationship with adult stepchildren, based on their own mutual interests rather than on their family ties. One stepmother has maintained a long and rewarding friendship with her stepson, even after she and his father divorced. They are both artists and have shared studio space. When her stepson and his wife's house burned, they lived with her for a period of time. She feels that her relationship with them is an important part of her life, something that was not dissolved when her marriage was. Ideally, as outlined in chapter 5, the final stage in stepfamily life is when the stepparent and the stepchildren have been able to establish a satisfying relationship that is separate from the marriage. Perhaps only Pollyanna would see the return of an adult child to the home as a golden opportunity to establish a warm, satisfying relationship between stepmother and stepchild, but it is not a bad ideal to keep in mind.

Like other passages in life, the marriage of a stepchild poses certain problems that are unique to stepfamilies. It's as though the family is suddenly "onstage," and is being observed by family and friends to see how everyone will behave. Many stepmothers have indicated that the fiancée's family is often the most uncomfortable and nervous about what to do with stepmothers. I certainly found that to be true when Lee's son Willy married.

The bride's family did not know what to do with me, so they solved the problem by largely ignoring me. I felt like a nonmember of the wedding. The most unsettling example of this was that when we entered the church, all of the female family members—except me—were given corsages to wear. Willy's mother was seated in the first row, alone, and I was put in the row behind. Lee sat with me, but when both sets of parents were called to stand behind the married couple, it was clear that I was to remain seated. I was allowed only to be an observer, not a participant.

With Lee's daughter, Kate, the situation is different. We are in the process of planning her wedding and the overall feeling among those involved is that it should be a happy day for all. Kate and I have enjoyed working and planning together and we have reached an accord with Kate's mother on most aspects of the celebration. It is perhaps indicative of the time we have spent together as a stepfamily, and of the fact that Kate and I have our own personal fondness for each other to draw on, that these plans are running so smoothly.

Stepmothers are usually at the mercy of the bride and her family, since they are the ones who plan the wedding. If the bride is the stepdaughter and has a good relationship with her stepmother, arrangements can be such that no one is left out or uncomfortable.

Beth, whose stepdaughter married recently, describes how well a wedding can go, even with the fears and tensions present whenever families and stepfamilies come together. At the rehearsal dinner given by the groom's family, she and her husband were placed at the opposite end of the room from the biological mother, who had not remarried. She could feel the tension in the room and felt as though everyone were watching to see how they would act toward one another. What Beth found most heartwarming, however, was the obvious intention on the part of her two stepchildren to help smooth things over. Her stepdaughter toasted her as well as her biological mother. Her stepson also included her in his toast. They both seemed to go out of their way to make sure she felt included and comfortable. The situation was not one in which she or her husband had much control, so the role of the children was extremely important. By acting "normal" and treating her like a relative, they diffused a potentially tense situation. At the wedding, she was escorted in after her stepdaughter's mother and before the groom's mother. The two mothers sat in the same pew, but with enough room between them so that when Beth's husband had given his daughter in marriage, he sat between them. By making these arrangements, Beth's stepdaughter gave her a special place in the ceremony. As Beth said, "Instead of feeling like an afterthought, I felt like the 'second mother' to my stepdaughter. It was a wonderful compliment."

Although a stepmother cannot always count on her step-children to understand and be sensitive to her situation at their weddings, it may be helpful for her to talk with them as plans are being made. As wonderful as weddings can be, they are also filled with anxiety and nervousness. Stepmothers can be easily overlooked or ignored when children are focusing on the details of the celebration. If a stepmother knows what's ahead and can prepare herself, she can better enjoy a day that should be a happy one for all. Talking to her stepchildren is easier than talking to the ex-wife, or to the family of the fiancée, and can be a time to strengthen the bond between her and her stepchild.

"The game's not over until it's over," the popular quote says—but families are never "over." Families remain families as long as there are family members, and the passages, trials, and celebrations of family life will continue to bring rewards, rejections, and sometimes relief.

13

In Praise of Stepmothers

RECENTLY LEE AND I CELEBRATED OUR TWENTY-FIRST WEDDING ANNI-versary. Soon our last child, Miranda, will be in college and we will be alone for the first time in our married life. We feel ready, although we will miss Miranda just as we missed the other children when they left. But we both feel that our child-rearing years, the phase of life when the family energies are concentrated on being a "family with kids," are over.

After thirty years of child-raising, I feel that it has been an extraordinarily wonderful period of my life, but it is now coming to an end. I am ready for a more peaceful, contemplative time. I want to concentrate on my life with Lee, on my work, and on pleasant times with friends, which will include my children. I find myself more able to enjoy them now as people, especially my stepchildren. It is easier for a stepmother than for a biological mother to view her stepchildren as friends rather than as children. I would be proud to claim Pete, Willy, and Kate as my children, but the fact that they are not my children makes me able to see and appreciate them with an objectivity a real parent would find more difficult. I know, because my feelings about Kristin are different: I worry about her, and think about what I was unable to do for her in the past. I have a much harder time separating from her. At the same time, I watch Lee appreciate Kristin, admiring her for her staunch individuality and seeing her just as she is, much as I am able to see his children.

As I look back on my life as a stepmother, there are things I wish I had done differently. I wish I had been more aware of others' feelings. I could have been more tolerant and perhaps more generous. Living in a family of "his, mine, and ours," I sometimes became overly preoccupied with mine and ours. I did not always understand what it was like to be a stepchild and although I liked Lee's children and tried to be nice to them, I could have had more empathy for their feelings. I can't pinpoint what was lacking, but I suspect this is a feeling many stepparents have. When Kristin was home recently and we were sitting together around the kitchen table, Lee suddenly looked at her and said, "Kris, the greatest regret of my life is that I wasn't a better stepfather to you." I knew exactly what he meant, because I have the same feelings. Perhaps as stepparents, we all ask too much of ourselves and blame ourselves too often. Since we don't know what we are supposed to feel, we judge ourselves by the only standard available.

I wish there had been two of me. I could have used a double. I always had too many things to do, and some things were therefore neglected. I often felt that I never got to spend as much time as I would have liked with any of the children or with Lee. Time is hard to find in a family that is constantly trying to deal with so many different needs. Now that I have the luxury of talking to one child at a time, I can appreciate how valuable it is.

I wish we had gotten professional help sooner. A wise family therapist can help sort out confusing and painful issues in a stepfamily, but we didn't discover one until well into our stepfamily life.

I wish we had worked out a better relationship with Lee's ex-wife. Now I see how much better it is for children to have parents who are cordial and cooperative. It should have been more of a priority in my life. Allowing my anger to overshadow their welfare was a disservice to them.

Nevertheless, I have never wished I was not a member of a stepfamily. The rewards have far outstripped the problems. My stepchildren mean a great deal to me, and I feel a sense of pride in being a member of such an interesting and varied family—a family of artists, builders, cooks, gardeners, and struggling actors and writers. Although Kristin and Willy tend to stay on the periphery of our family, we all keep in contact, and we all *feel* like a family when we get together. Looking back through our photograph albums, I see us going through each stage: our first years together, babies arriving, adolescents blooming, and hair graying. The smiling faces caught by the camera seem to reflect untroubled happiness. Painful moments are not visibly chronicled, but they exist in our collective memory. That collective memory includes many things that we have gone through, good and bad, and the knowledge that we have gone through it together. The years have forged a bond between us that nothing can alter. Like Pinocchio becoming a real boy, our stepfamily has become a "real family."

But this process has taken time, and in spite of the rewards, I know what stepmothers mean when they express their difficulties.

"Being a stepmother is the hardest thing I've ever tried to do."

Almost every stepmother interviewed made this statement in one way or another. Being a stepmother *is* one of the hardest things to do, and most stepmothers have tried to find their way feeling at times isolated and without guidelines. They have entered their stepmother lives with the best of intentions and a genuine desire to live a fulfilling life with their husbands and their stepchildren. Nevertheless, it is a rare stepmother who has found her role fulfilling without a struggle. Good intentions and high hopes are not enough to carry the stepfamily through the years of adjustment necessary to form a family bond. Stepmothers also need much support, and an understanding that the supreme task they have undertaken is filled with complexities.

Society should give stepmothers credit for this undertaking, and stepmothers should give credit to themselves. Our stereotypical image of the wicked stepmother must give way to a more positive image of resourceful, valiant women taking on the building of a new and growing family unit in our society. In spite of the cultural changes over the past few decades, mothers are still of primary importance in the family structure, and by the sheer number of stepfamilies being formed (almost 1,300 a day) it is a fact that stepmothers play a pivotal role in contemporary society.

Most important, stepmothers must have a positive image of themselves. Both individually and collectively, stepmothers need to put away the old prejudices and to see themselves as brave pioneers on a new frontier. The age of Aquarius may be over, but one can herald the dawning of the age of stepfamilies. Like any other new social phenomenon it is heralded with forebodings by some and seen as an exciting challenge by others. As the number of people involved in this change increases, language will catch up, support systems will grow, and a new and more sympathetic understanding by society as a whole will develop.

An aspect of this new phenomenon that makes it different from other social changes is the persistent though outdated negative image of the stepmother. In looking through various collections of familiar quotations, there is not a single one that has anything good to say about a stepmother. There is, however, in contemporary American society a romantic image of the stepmother as a wonderful, cheerful, beautiful woman who captures the love of a bitter father and his ten children. She is brave in the face of danger, cheerful in the face of disappointment, and resourceful in the face of need. This stepmother not only rescues her family from the tyrannies of a regimented household but also saves them from Nazi oppression. This amazing stepmother is Julie Andrews as Maria Von Trapp in *The Sound of Music*, one of the most popular film musicals of this century.

The movie is, of course, in many ways as unrealistic as a fairy tale, but perhaps just because it is filled with so much brave optimism and cheerfulness, we all want to believe it. The continuing popularity of this musical implies a collective hope in the ability to overcome adversity through optimism and steadfast nurturing. What stepmother has not had the fantasy of being like Maria—happy, cheerful, caring, and brave. Selfless.

The fact that Maria came to the Von Trapp family from a convent makes her atypical of the average stepmother, but since many nuns are trained to care for other people's children, and the term "mother" is widely used in the Catholic community, it is interesting to see how their training is applicable for stepmothers.

One woman interviewed was a nun for thirty years before she left the order to marry a man with four children. Her early experience as a nun enabled her to take on the tasks of stepfamily life with amazing fortitude and equanimity. Although her situation is unique, her story is both interesting and informative.

Trained through rigorous discipline to be selfless, Sarah's purpose in life was dedication to the Church manifested through service to others. When she was young, she taught in a Catholic boarding school. She slept in the same room with twenty young girls and with no separate space for herself. She had no privacy and expected none. Even her few clothes were kept in a small trunk by her cot.

She was called "Mother" by the girls and she was expected to play the role of mother and guide to her charges. Although she was responsible for the girls' discipline, she was also in charge of seeing that their individual needs were addressed— everything from an extra blanket or warm cup of milk at night to being available to comfort and talk to them when they were troubled. She was dedicating her life to other people's children and she knew they would pass on through her life to a life of their own. She did not expect these children to thank her, for her rewards came from a higher order, something beyond the gratification of the girls in her charge.

When Sarah became a stepmother, her early training stood her in good stead. Her husband's children were older but had grown up in the tumultuous sixties and had experienced the trauma of parental conflict and divorce. Sarah knew she could never be their mother or even play a mothering role with these older children. Her commitment to them was definite, however. She loved their father and was determined always to make them feel welcome in his home, no matter how difficult the circumstances. Sarah's sense of selflessness and her deep faith enabled her to see that although life can be hard, it is made meaningful by making it easier for other people. When her stepchildren needed time, money, or space in her home, she gave to them willingly. She felt that no matter how much she thought *she* was unhappy with the actions of her stepchildren, her husband suffered more because he was their father. Her goal was to help him.

Sarah also had a clear perception of her role as a woman. She was convinced that women are different from men in that they are more intuitive about other people's problems and can sense the needs of others more perceptively. Her intuitive qualities were important in helping her husband and his children work through their problems. Her stepchildren were drawn to her understanding nature, and there have been times when Sarah has been the only one in touch with all the family members. Some of her experiences would try the patience of a saint, but she speaks of her life with her stepfamily in terms of steadfast commitment and continued hope for the future.

Sarah's attitude as a stepmother is educational. First and foremost, she believes that a father must never be separated from his children by his wife. She also believes that fulfillment is found in trying to make life better for other people, and that this giving must be for itself, not based on a need for appreciation.

Partly because of her nature and religious commitment, she has found stepmothering an enriching experience. Few of us are prepared, however, by nature or by training, to be as selfless and giving. Sarah sees her own experience as being individual and not even necessarily ideal. She is the first to maintain that you cannot demand something of yourself that you cannot do, and that no person is well served by trying to conform to an unrealistic ideal. Her philosophy is one that every stepmother should keep in mind, however. Much pain and adversity can be avoided if a stepmother never forgets that she married a father, and that his relationship with his children must be respected and nurtured.

Secondly, although trying to be the selfless "super-mom-stepmother" can lead to frustration and anger, an appropriate dedication to the needs and welfare of her family can give a stepmother inner satisfaction. It is the ability to give without expecting specific rewards, in terms of appreciation or behavior, that is worth striving for. Stepfamilies, like biological families, do not work on a quid pro quo basis, although things usually balance out in the long run, even if the balance is only the stepmother knowing in her heart that she did the best she could.

The two images of stepmothering—wicked stepmother versus saint—are important because they underscore the two extremes that create the fears and fantasies of many stepmothers. Between the two archetypes are millions of stepmothers struggling to establish their own individual identity. Indicative of this movement is the search for adequate language to describe the relationships and interworkings of stepfamily life. Although therapists, journalists, and media experts try to apply terms to stepfamily relationships, it is the family members themselves who will develop a language and a new way of perceiving themselves. The search for terms that "fit" is emblematic of our search to define the complexities of this new family unit. We create perceptions through our language, and in interviewing numerous stepmothers, it was both interesting and heartening to hear the original and perceptive ways in which they described their situations. There was a definite effort to create a more positive image of the stepfamily rather than allow the old negative images to hold them back. There is a "spirit" of stepmothering, almost a tangible movement of many women moving ahead with their lives and being willing to take risks and create new and better realities. This "stepmother spirit" distinguishes itself in its earnestness, and it is alive and growing.

Although being a stepmother is hard and at times debilitating, not a single stepmother interviewed did not have a positive contribution to make toward this book. Individually, the stepmothers have found ways not only to cope with but to enrich their experience. Collectively, they have presented interesting and helpful methods of living life as a stepmother. Both in their struggles and in their victories, stepmothers used clear and innovative images to tell their stories.

The frustrations and longings of stepmothers were expressed regularly. Such comments as "not living life on your own terms," "inheriting other people's problems," "losing the marriage in family life," or "too many takers from the common pot" all indicated the difficulties stepmothers encounter. Many stepmothers spoke of their yearning for a "normal married life." One young stepmother who married a man with four older children described her feelings when she saw a young married couple with their toddler: "They were walking down the street with their ice creams. The couple were arm in arm, pushing a stroller with their little boy. The father bent down and gave him a bite of ice cream and he kicked his little feet, which were turned inward. I wanted to be a family like that!"

The family she saw with the parents walking slowly together, enjoying their only child, separate from the outside world but not alone, looked contentedly uncomplicated. It was what she had always envisioned as the young family. It doesn't seem like so much to ask for, but it is everything a stepfamily is not.

All of the images and descriptions were not negative, however. With so little tradition and so few positive analogies existing in our culture, stepmothers were also creative in finding positive analogies to their situations. Stepmothers defined themselves in a variety of ways—as mentor, friend, female role model, guide, aunt. Many tried to be a constant in the lives of children experiencing turmoil and change.

They described their families as "families of choice," "made-up families," and "enlarged or extended families." One stepmother found the idea of her stepfamily being different from a nuclear family helpful. As she saw it, a nuclear family is all of one piece with members circling around a central core, whereas a stepfamily is made up of different pieces carefully fitted together through trial and error, but stronger because of the separate bonding.

Sally, who is an actress, compared her stepfamily to an acting ensemble. As in an ensemble, there is an active collaboration and an exchange between members. Although the script has been written and everyone has a role to play, only by exploring beneath the official roles can the actors bring forth their best and most convincing performances. Even the most well-known dramatic characters can be reinterpreted by a great actor. Part of the process is first finding out what the questions are in the situation and then trying to answer them. It is when the actors stop playing a role and become that character that the play works. The motto for actors is, "Don't play the king—*be* the king."

The stepfamily is like the acting ensemble in that it has been given the outline of a role to play; everyone comes to the stepfamily production with his or her own bag of tricks; and the success of the stepfamily does rely on its members' ability to explore their roles, ask the right questions, and confront the ensemble as a whole in order to fulfill their roles satisfactorily. Also just like a stage production, stepfamilies often feel that they are being observed, and there are critics out there who will be quick to point out failings.

By viewing her stepfamily in terms of her experience as an actress, Sally finds it easier to work through problems and move forward. It not only gives her much-needed distance from the daily hassles but also bolsters her need to believe that things will work out. As she says, "You always think a production won't make it; there are so many obstacles in the way. But by working on it day in and day out, the big night finally comes and you make it a success."

The variety of ways of viewing stepfamily life implies that there is no official list of rules to guarantee successful stepmothering. Stepfamily life is simply too complicated, and each family is unique. Stepfamilies have a past, a present, and a future life that affects every day of their existence.

Stepfamilies are not isolated units but extend far beyond the boundaries of a biological family. They have a cast of characters involved in their life over which no one has control. They are also affected by greater outside forces, societal or legal, which make life more problematic. At the same time, the stepfamily involves a number of people who are emotionally, legally, psychologically, and financially bound together in some way but are not biologically kin. No other social unit is so complex.

In dealing with this complex unit, there are two basic things a stepmother can do: seek support from the outside, and find strength and solace inside herself. Outside support comes from husbands, children, friends, therapists, and organized groups. Inside strength is less easy to define.

A satisfying relationship with her husband is the stepmother's most important source of outside support. "Together we stand, divided we fall" is a truism for couples in stepfamilies. Even when the marriage is barraged by conflicting forces, every effort should be made to keep the marriage alive. A woman needs to be committed to her marriage and willing to defend this commitment if necessary. Although her choice of spouse affects both her own children and her stepchildren, she has both a right to this choice and a need to stick by it. She needs to believe in herself enough to stand by her husband. One stepmother whose children were unhappy when she married her second husband had to make a clear statement to them.

"There is no choice," she announced. "You *have* to work it out with Edward. He is my husband and I will remain with him."

She was convinced that her husband, although difficult at times for her children, was a person who would enrich their lives in the long run. Her fierce defense of her husband eventually resulted in a close-knit stepfamily.

Another mother saw her second marriage as a good

example for her children and stepchildren: "By our loving each other and being committed to each other, our children saw that marriage *could* work."

My daughter Kristin maintains that my relationship with Lee has been an example she wants to follow. She sees our relationship as one that is still evolving, full of excitement and change but based on a loving commitment.

Many problems that seem insurmountable can be survived when a couple remain committed to each other. If there is one primary source of strength for a stepmother, it is a good marriage. It is worth working for.

Children can also be a great source of comfort and support—both biological children and stepchildren. One stepmother, when asked if she could be interviewed, responded, "Yes, but you really need to interview my partner as well. He and I have been through it all together." She was referring to her stepson.

Every mother interviewed could recall incidents in which her children and stepchildren helped her, often in unexpected ways. Children almost always want there to be harmony in their home and given a chance they will work with their parents and stepparents toward it—if not all the time, at least some of the time. Children also receive genuine satisfaction if they can be helpful. Thinking of one's children and stepchildren as partners, a possible source of support, rather than as adversaries can do more good than harm.

Stepmothers often turn to friends, although they usually feel that only other stepmothers can understand. Stepfamily resource centers are being formed through psychological counseling centers and churches, and are becoming more common. The Stepfamily Association of America, with its growing number of chapters and its bulletins, is also an excellent resource. Stepmothers show innovation in looking for help, from joining Alcoholics Anonymous to going to silent retreats where they can just be alone and quiet for a few days or hours. Also, just as women came together to form consciousness-raising groups in the sixties and seventies, women are beginning to join together to discuss stepmothering.

Therapists are another source of support and have worked with many stepmothers. Although psychologists only really have begun to concentrate on stepfamily problems, more and more professionals are being trained in this area. Therapists tend to be open to new methods and ideas on treating the stepfamily, and many women have found their time spent in therapy especially helpful.

In the final analysis, however, it is the inner resources of each individual woman that will be most important in helping her as a stepmother. Like other challenges in life, being a stepmother can bring out strengths in a woman that even she did not know she had. In interviewing many stepmothers at length, I was always heartened by the valor of the human spirit. Stepmothers are amazing! They are resourceful, they strive to be honest, they try to find humor in life, and they possess an earnestness that shows they are really alive. None of them could say that her life was boring or dull.

Qualities that stepmothers themselves believe have helped them are a sense of humor, honesty, steadfastness, and above all hope that things will work out.

A sense of humor does not mean that a stepmother needs to be able to tell jokes, but that she needs to find the humor that almost always exists in the human situation. A sense of humor not only helps alleviate troubles but also gives a pleasing dimension to everyday life.

A friend of the Duke and Duchess of Windsor was interviewed when the duchess died. When asked what it was about the duchess that made her so appealing that the duke gave up his crown to marry her, she replied, "It wasn't that she was particularly beautiful or intelligent. But she had a wit about her ... she made the duke laugh. You know, it is a wonderful thing to laugh."

To be able to laugh, to find humor in everyday occurrences, gives warmth and pleasure to life. As Thackeray says in *Sketches, Love, Marriage,* "A good laugh is sunshine in a house." There are few events that have not one whit of humor in them, if only one is able to see it.

Another quality seen as invaluable is honesty. As one

therapist said, "An honest relationship is an honest relationship. It will survive." Honesty is also being true to one's self. Stepmothers often struggle with this, trying to understand their own actions and reactions to other family members. It is not so much that stepmothers can always be honest, but it is important that they strive to be.

Steadfastness is a quality that is not dramatic and certainly is not romantic. It is not even something one can point to at a given time. It is long-term, patient, and steady. Steadfastness is sometimes just enduring . . . and hoping that this too shall pass away. A stepmother must realize that creating a healthy stepfamily takes time, usually years. It is the multitude of days spent actively working toward unity that will eventually create a family.

It is her steadfastness of vision, her hope for the future, and her commitment to her husband and family that the stepmother must draw on over and over again. Taking it one step at a time requires steadfastness, but it is the only way a stepfamily can evolve into a satisfying unit.

Above the entrance to hell in Dante's *Inferno* is written, "Abandon all hope ye who enter here." Life without hope, and a stepfamily without hope or a vision of progress, can also be hell. A Bible verse says, "Where there is no vision, the people perish." As the mother in a family, a stepmother's vision is essential. Falling short of ideals does not negate the need for a hope or vision of these ideals. Hope for the best, and meanwhile do the best you can. That's all you can do.

A tribute was once made to a stepmother by one of the most honored men in American history. "All that I am or hope to be I owe to my angel mother," Abraham Lincoln said, in reference to Sarah Bush Lincoln, who became his stepmother when he was ten years old.

This man saw his stepmother as the greatest influence on his life. Although few stepmothers can expect such a tribute, or expect to influence the course of human events by being a stepmother, it is nice to know that the positive influence of stepmothering has a place in American history.

There have been stepmothers since the beginning of time.

But today, more than at any other time in history, stepmothers must play a role in society that will, collectively, affect the course of human events. Being a stepmother may be the most difficult thing in the world to do, but it can also be the most important.

Notes

CHAPTER 2

1. Joan B. Kelly and Judith S. Wallerstein, "The Effects of Parental Divorce: Experiences of the Child in Early Latency," *American Journal of Orthopsychiatry* 46 no. 1 (1976): 20–42.

2. Jean Rosenbaum and Veryl Rosenbaum, *Stepparenting* (Corte Madera, Calif.: Chandler and Sharp Publishers, Inc., 1977), p. 20.

3. Ibid., p. 23.

4. Emily B. Visher and John S. Visher, *Stepfamilies: A Guide to Working with Stepparents and Stepchildren* (New York: Brunner/Mazel, 1979), p. 261.

CHAPTER 3

1. Judith Martin, *Miss Manners' Guide to Excruciatingly Correct Behavior* (New York: Atheneum, 1982), p. 338.

2. Ibid., p. 573.

CHAPTER 4

1. Jessie Bernard, *The Future of Marriage* (New Haven: Yale University Press, 1982), p. 243.

2. Ibid., p. 241.

3. Linda Bird Francke, *Growing Up Divorced* (New York: Simon and Schuster, Linden Press, 1983), p. 44.

CHAPTER 5

1. Bruno Bettelheim, *The Uses of Enchantment: The Meaning and Importance of Fairy Tales* (New York: Alfred A. Knopf, 1976), p. 5.

2. Ibid., p. 8.

3. Patricia Lee Papernow, "A Phenomenological Study of the Developmental Stages of Becoming a Stepparent—a Gestalt and Family Systems Approach" (Ann Arbor, Mich.: University Microfilms International, 1980).

4. Boston Women's Health Book Collective, *Ourselves and Our Children* (New York: Random House, 1978), p. 156.

5. Sonya Rhodes, *Surviving Family Life: The Seven Crises of Living Together* (New York: G. P. Putnam's Sons, 1981), p. 170.

6. Papernow, p. 238.

CHAPTER 8

1. Sue Hubbell, *A Country Year: Living the Question* (New York: Random House, 1986), p. 90.

2. David M. Mills, "A Model for Stepfamily Development," *Family Relations* Vol. 33 (July 1984): 369.

3. Helen Thomson, *The Successful Stepparent* (New York: Funk & Wagnalls, 1966), p. 137.

4. Mills, p. 369.

CHAPTER 9

1. Dr. Bruce A. Baldwin, "Puberty and Parents: Understanding Your Early Adolescent," *Piedmont Airlines Magazine* (October 1986): 13–20.

CHAPTER 10

1. Ashley Montagu, *Touching: The Human Significance of the Skin* (New York: Harper & Row, 1978), pp. 161–62.

2. Dr. Sonya Rhodes, *Surviving Family Life: The Seven Crises of Living Together* (New York: G. P. Putnam's Sons, 1981), p. 151.

3. Jean Giles-Sims and David Finkelhor, "Child Abuse in Stepfamilies," *Family Relations,* vol. 33 (July 1984): 411.

4. Ibid., p. 410.

5. Clifford J. Sager et al., *Treating the Remarried Family* (New York: Brunner/Mazel, 1983), p. 303.

6. David M. Mills, "A Model for Stepfamily Development," Family Relations, vol. 33 (July 1984): 371.

Bibliography

Atkin, Edith, and Rubin, Estelle. *Part-Time Father*. New York: Vanguard, 1976.

Baer, Jean. *The Second Wife*. New York: Doubleday, 1972.

Baldwin, Bruce. "Puberty and Parents: Understanding Your Early Adolescent." *Piedmont Airlines Magazine* (October 1986): pp. 13–20.

Berman, Claire. *Making It as a Stepparent*. New York: Doubleday, 1980.

—. *Stepfamilies—A Growing Reality*. Washington, D.C.: Department of Health, Education and Welfare, Public Affairs Pamphlet 609 (1982).

Bernard, Jessie. *The Future of Marriage*. New Haven: Yale University Press, 1982.

Bettelheim, Bruno. *The Uses of Enchantment: The Meaning and Importance of Fairy Tales*. New York: Alfred A. Knopf, 1976.

Bitterman, Catherine. "The Multi-Marriage Family." *Social Casework* 49 (1968): 218–221.

Bohannan, Paul, and Erickson, Rosemary. "Stepping In." *Psychology Today,* (January 1978): 53.

Boston Women's Health Book Collective. *Ourselves and Our Children: A Book by and for Children.* New York: Random House, 1978.

Bowen, M. *Family Therapy in Clinical Practice.* New York: Jason Aronson, 1978.

Bowerman, Charles E., and Irish, Donald P. "Some Relationships of Stepchildren to Their Parents." *Marriage and Family Living,* 24 (1962): 113–21.

Bowlby, J. *Attachment and Loss.* New York: Basic Books, Inc., 1969.

Brand, Eulalee. "The Interdependence of Intrafamiliar Dyads: Marital Quality and Parent-Child Relationships." Ph.D. dissertation, Temple University. Ann Arbor, Mich.: University Microfilms International, 1985.

Brooks, Andree. "Stepchildren Panel Tell Parents How It Is." *New York Times* (January 13, 1985): 46.

———. "Becoming an 'Instant' Stepmother." *New York Times* (August 4, 1986): 14.

———. "Stepparents and Divorce: Keeping Ties to Children." *New York Times* (July 29, 1984): 46.

Brown, Martha C. "A Special Kind of Help for Children of Divorce." *Family Weekly* (June 1983): 10.

Burchinal, L. G. "Characteristics of Adolescents from Unbroken, Broken, and Reconstructed Families." *Journal of Marriage and the Family* 26 (1964): 44–51.

Burns, Cherie. "How to Survive Without Feeling Frustrated, Left Out, or Wicked." New York: Times Books, 1985.

Carter, E. A., and McGoldrick, M. *The Family Life Cycle: A Framework for Family Therapy.* New York: Gardner Press, 1980.

Center for Family Learning. *The Best of Family*. Compilation of Selected papers and articles from *The Family*, 1973–78, New Rochelle, N.Y.: Center for Family Learning, Eileen G. Pendagast, editor.

Chess, Stella, and Thomas, Alexander. *Annual Progress in Child Psychiatry and Child Development*. 12 vols. New York: Brunner-Mazel.

Clingempeel, W. Glen, Brand, Eulalee, and Ievoli, Richard. "Stepparent-Stepchild Relationships in Stepmother and Stepfather Families: A Multimethod Study." *Family Relations* 33 (1984): 465–473.

Collins, Glenn. "Remarriage: Bigger Ready-Made Families." *New York Times* (May 13, 1985): B5.

————. "Stepfamilies Share their Joys and Woes." *New York Times* (October 24, 1983): 45.

Crosbie-Burnett, M. "The Centrality of the Step Relationship: A Challenge to Family Theory and Practice." *Family Relations* 33 (1984): 459–464.

Demaris, Alfred. "A Comparison of Remarriages with First Marriages or Satisfaction in Marriage and its Relationship to Prior Cohabitation." *Family Relations* 33 (1984): 443–447.

Despert, J. Louise. *Children of Divorce*. New York: Doubleday, 1953.

Dodson, Fitzhugh. "Weaving Together Two Families into One." *Family Health* no. 9 (1977): 44–51, 51–52.

Draughton, Margaret. "Stepmother's Role of Identification In Relation to Mourning in the Child." *Psychological Reports* 36 (1975): 183–89.

Duberman, Lucile. "Step-Kin Relationships." *Journal of Marriage and The Family* 35 (May 1973): 283–95.

Duffin, Sharyn R. "Yours, Mine and Ours: Tips for Stepparents." U.S. Department of Health, Education and Welfare, publication no. (ADM) 78-676 (1978).

Dullea, Georgia. "Stepparents Pressing for Custody Rights as New Legal Issue." *New York Times* (March 2, 1987): 45.

Einstein, Elizabeth. *The Stepfamily: Living, Loving and Learning.* New York: MacMillan Publishing Co. Inc., 1982.

Fast, Irene, and Cain, Albert C. "The Stepparent Role." *American Journal of Orthopsychiatry* 36 (1966): 485–91.

Ferber, Andrew; Mendelsohn, Marilyn; and Napier, August. *The Book of Family Therapy.* Boston: Houghton Mifflin Co., 1972.

Fields, Suzanne. *Like Father, Like Daughter: How Father Shapes the Woman His Daughter Becomes.* Boston: Little, Brown and Co., 1983.

Francke, Linda Bird. *Growing Up Divorced.* New York: Simon and Schuster, Linden Press, 1983.

Framo, James L. "The Friendly Divorce." *Psychology Today* (February 1978): 77.

Freud, Sigmund. *The Major Works of Sigmund Freud: Great Books of the Western World.* Ed. by Robert Maynard Hutchins. Chicago: Encyclopaedia Britannica, Inc., 1952.

Giles-Sims, Jean, and Finkelhor, David. "Child Abuse in Stepfamilies." *Family Relations* (July 1984): 407–413.

Glenn, Norval, and Weaver, Charles. "The Marital Happiness of Remarried Divorced Persons." *Journal of Marriage and the Family* (May 1977): 331.

Goetting, A. "The Six Stations of Remarriage: Developmental Tasks of Remarriage After Divorce." *Family Relations* (April 1982): 213–222.

Goldman, Janice, and Coane, James. "Family Therapy After the Divorce." *Family Process* 16 (1977): 357–362.

Guerin, P. J. *Family Therapy.* New York: Gardner Press, 1976.

Haley, J. *Problem Solving Therapy.* New York: Harper & Row, 1976.

Hubbell, Sue. *A Country Year: Living the Questions.* New York: Random House, 1986.

Jacobson, D. S. "Stepfamilies: Myths and Realities." *Social Work* 24 no. 3 (May 1979): 202–207.

Kagan, Jerome. "The Parental Love Trap." *Psychology Today* (August 1978): 54–91.

Kalter, Suzy. *Instant Parent.* New York: A & W, 1979.

Kaplan, Stuart. "Structural Family Therapy for Children of Divorce: Case Reports." *Family Process* 16 (1977): 75–83.

Keniston, Kenneth, and the Carnegie Council on Children. *All Our Children: The American Family Under Pressure.* New York and London: Harcourt Brace Jovanovich, 1977.

Klienman, J.; Rosenberg, E.; and Whiteside, M. "Common Developmental Tasks in Forming Reconstituted Families." *Journal of Marital and Family Therapy* 2, no. 5 (April 1979): 79–86.

Krantzler, Mel. *Creative Divorce.* New York: New American Library, 1975.

Lasch, Christopher. *The Culture of Narcissism: American Life in an Age of Diminishing Expectations.* New York: W. W. Norton & Co., Inc., 1978.

Levinger, George, and Moles, Oliver C. *Divorce and Separation: Context, Causes, and Consequences.* New York: Basic Books, Inc., 1979.

Lippincott, Mary Ann. "Stepfamily Integration: A Study of Stepfamily Issues and Their Impact on Stepfamily Environment." Ph.D dissertation, University of Connecticut. Ann Arbor, Mich.: University Microfilms International, 1985.

Lofas, Jeanette, with Sova, Dawn. *Step-Parenting: A Complete Guide to the Joys, Frustrations, and Fears of Stepparenting!* New York: Zebra, N.U.G., 1985.

Louie, Elaine. "The Newest Extended Family." *House and Garden* (August 1987): 16.

Lovett, Luis. "Stepmothering: Am I Ready For This?" MS (November 1982): 114.

Lowe, Patricia Tracy. *The Cruel Stepmother.* Englewood Cliffs, N.J.: Prentice-Hall, Inc., 1970.

Maddox, Brenda. *The Half-Parent.* New York: Evans, 1975.

Martin, Judith. *Miss Manners' Guide to Excruciatingly Correct Behavior.* New York: Atheneum, 1982.

Mayleas, Davidyn. *Rewedded Bliss.* New York: Basic Books, Inc., 1977.

McClenahan, Carolyn. "Sensitive Issues in Stepparenting." Unpublished article (1977).

Messinger, Lillian; Walker, Kenneth N.; and Freeman, Stanley J. J. "Preparation for Remarriage Following Divorce: The Use of Group Techniques." *American Journal of Orthopsychiatry* 48 No. 2 (April 1978): 263–272.

Miller, Sue. *The Good Mother.* New York: Harper & Row, 1986.

Mills, D. "A Model for Stepfamily Development." *Family Relations* 33 (July 1984): 365–372.

Minuchin, S. *Families and Family Therapy.* Cambridge, Mass.: Harvard University Press, 1974.

Montagu, Ashley. *Touching: The Human Significance of the Skin.* New York: Harper & Row, 1978.

Morris, Lorna Jean. "A Comparison Of Marital Satisfaction and Stepfamily Integration in Stepmother and Stepfather Remarriages." Ph.D. dissertation, U.S. International University. Ann Arbor, Mich.: University Microfilms International, 1985.

Nadler, J. H. "The Psychological Stress of Stepmothers." Ph.D. dissertation. Abstracts International April 1977, *37* C10-B S367-B No. 77-6308.

Napier, A. Y. *The Family Crucible.* New York: Harper & Row, 1978.

Noble, June, and Nobel, William. *How to Live with Other People's Children.* New York: Hawthorn Books, 1979.

Nye, F. Ivan. "Child Adjustment in Broken and in Unbroken Homes." *Marriage and Family Living* (November 1957): 356–360.

Olson, David; Russel, Candyce; and Sprenkel, Douglas. "Marital and Family Therapy." *Journal of Marriage and the Family* (November 1980): 965–968.

Papernow, Patricia Lee. "A Phenomenological Study of the Developmental Stages of Becoming a Stepparent—A Gestalt and Family Systems Approach." Ph.D. dissertation. Ann Arbor, Mich.: University Microfilms International, 1980.

————. "The Stepfamily Cycle: An Experimental Model of Stepfamily Development." *Family Relations* 33:355–363.

Parke, Ross D. *The Developing Child.* Cambridge, Mass.: Harvard University Press, 1981.

Perez, Joseph. *Family Counseling.* Van Nostrand Reinhold Co., 1979.

Pfloger, Janet. "The Wicked Stepmother in a Child Guidance Clinic." *The Personnel and Guidance Journal* (March 1982): 393–397.

Price-Papillo, Thelma Jean. "The Visited Stepfamily: A Preliminary Inquiry." Ph.D. dissertation, the Fielding Institute, Ann Arbor, Mich.: University Microfilms International, 1985.

Ransom, J. W.; Schlesinger, S.; and Derdeyn, A. P. "A Stepfamily in Formation." *American Journal of Orthopsychiatry* 49 no. 1 (January 1979): 36–43.

Reingold, Carmel Berman. *Remarriage.* New York: Harper & Row, 1976.

Remarriage periodical, Boston: G & R Publications Inc.

Rhodes, Sonya. *Surviving Family Life: The Seven Crises of Living Together.* New York: G. P. Putnam's Sons, 1981.

Ricks, Delthia. "Stepmothers Are Worried, Not Wicked, Study Says." *Atlanta Const. Journal* (October 10, 1980).

Roman, Mel and Haddad, William. "The Case for Joint Custody." *Psychology Today* (September 1978): 96–105.

Roosevelt, Ruth, and Lofas, Jeannette. *Living in Step.* New York: Stein & Day, Inc., 1976.

Rosenbaum, Jean, and Rosenbaum, Meryl. *Stepparenting.* New York: E. P. Dutton, Inc., 1977.

Rosenthal, Kristine M., and Keshet, Harry, F. "The Not-Quite Stepmother." *Psychology Today* (July 1978): 83–101.

Sager, Clifford, and Kaplan, Helen Singer. *Progress in Group and Family Therapy.* New York: Brunner/Mazel, 1972.

Sager, Clifford. *Treating the Remarried Family.* New York: Brunner/Mazel, 1983.

Sager, Clifford; Walker, Elizabeth; Brown, Hollis Steer; Crohn, Helen M.; and Rodstein, Evelyn. "Improved Functioning of the Remarried Family System." *Journal of Marital and Family Therapy* 7 no. 2 (January 1981): 3–11.

Sager, Clifford J.; Brown, Hollis Steer; Crohn, Helen; Enjee, Tamara; Rodstein, Evelyn, and Walker, Libby. *Treating the Remarried Family.* New York: Brunner/Mazel, 1983.

Sardanis-Zimmeran, I. "The Stepmother: Mythology and Self-Perception." Dissertation Abstracts International 38 (6B) 2884. (December 1977).

Satir, Virginia. *Peoplemaking.* Science and Behavior Books, Inc., 1972.

———. *Conjoint Family Therapy.* Science and Behavior Books, Inc., 1967.

Savage, Karen. "The Stepfamily: New Light Is Shed on an Old Notion." *New York Times* (April 8, 1984): 25.

———. "At Peace with Role as Stepmother." *New York Times* (March 8, 1981): 24.

Serritella, D. A. "Stepfathers, Stepdaughters: Sexual Issues in the Remarried Family." *American Journal of Family Therapy* 9 no. 4 (1981): 90–92.

Shulman, Gerda. "Myths That Intrude on the Adaptation of the Stepfamily." *Social Casework* 53 (1972): 131–39.

Simon, Anne W. *Stepchild in the Family,* Odyssey, 1964.

Smith, William. *The Stepchild.* Chicago: University of Chicago Press, 1953.

Smith, Robert Paul. *"Where Did You Go?" "Out." "What Did You Do?" "Nothing."* Macfadden Books, 1966.

Spann, Owen, and Spann, Marcie. *Your Child? I Thought It Was My Child!* Pasadena, Calif.: Ward Ritchie Press, 1977.

Thomson, Helen. *The Successful Stepparent.* New York: Harper & Row, 1968.

Tollison, C. David, and Adams, Henry E. *Sexual Disorders.* New York: Gardner Press, 1979.

Toman, Walter. *Family Constellation.* New York: Springer Publishing Company, 1961.

Turkington, Carol. "Stepfamilies." *Christian Science Monitor* (October 1984): 8.

Visher, Emily B. and Visher, John. *Stepfamilies.* New York: Brunner/Mazel, 1979.

———. *How to Win as a Stepfamily.* New York: Brunner/Mazel, 1982.

———. "Common Problems of Stepparents and Their Spouses." *American Journal of Orthopsychiatry* 48 (2) (April 1978): 252–61.

Wallerstein, Judith S., and Kelly, Joan B. *Surviving the Breakup: How Children Actually Cope with Divorce.* New York: Basic Books, Inc., 1980.

———. "California's Children of Divorce." *Psychology Today* (January 1980): 67–76.

———. "Children and Divorce: A Review." *Social Work* (November 1979): 468–474.

———. "The Effects of Parental Divorce: The Adolescent

Experience." *Journal of the Academy of Child Psychiatry* 14 (Autumn 1975): 600–616.

———. "The Effects of Parental Divorce: Experiences of the Child in Later Latency." *American Journal of Orthopsychiatry* (January 1976): 20–32.

———. "The Effects of Parental Divorce: Experiences of the Child in Early Latency." *American Journal of Orthopsychiatry* 46, (April 1976): 256–269.

Walter, K. N., and Messinger, L. "Remarriage After Divorce." *Family Process* 18 no. 2 (1979): 185–92.

Westoff, Leslie A. *The Second Time Around.* New York: Penguin Books, 1978.

Yoburg, Betty. *Families and Societies: Survival or Extinction?* New York: Columbia University Press, 1983.

Index